THE CULTURE

OF

COUNTER-CULTURE

THE EDITED TRANSCRIPTS

ALAN WATTS
at a seminar aboard the SS *Vallejo*, 1966

THE CULTURE

OF

COUNTER-CULTURE

THE EDITED TRANSCRIPTS

Charles E. Tuttle Co., Inc.
Boston ✦ Rutland, Vermont ✦ Tokyo

First paperback edition published in 1999 by Tuttle Publishing, an imprint of
Periplus Editions (HK) Ltd., with editorial offices at 153 Milk Street, Boston,
Massachusetts 02109.

Photo courtesy of Alan Watts Electronic Educational Programs

Library of Congress Cataloging-in-Publication Data

Watts, Alan, 1915–1973.
   The culture of counter-culture / Alan Watts.
      p. cm.–(The "love of wisdom" library)
    Contents: Mysticism and morality—On being God—What is reality?—
From time to eternity—The smell of burnt almonds—Philosophy of nature.
    ISBN 0-8048-3197-1 (pbk)
    1. Mysticism. 2. Philosophy. 3. Religion. 4. Ethics. 5. United States—
Moral conditions. 6. United States—Religion—1960- 7. United States—
Civilization—20th century. 8.Watts, Alan, 1915–1973. I. Title. II. Series:
Watts, Alan, 1915–1973. Alan Watts "love of wisdom" library.
BL625.T34   1998
191–dc21   98–18495
                                                                 CIP

Distributed by

USA
Tuttle Publishing
Distribution Center
Airport Industrial Park
364 Innovation Drive
North Clarendon, VT 05759-9436
Tel: (802) 773-8930
Fax: (802) 773-6993

SOUTHEAST ASIA
Berkeley Books Pte. Ltd.
5 Little Road #08-01
Singapore 536983
Tel: (65) 280-3320
Fax: (65) 280-6290

JAPAN
Tuttle Shokai Ltd.
1-21-13, Seki
Tama-ku, Kawasaki-shi
Kanagawa-ken 214, Japan
Tel: (044) 833-0225
Fax: (044) 822-0413

CANADA
Raincoast Books
8680 Canbie Street
Vancouver, British Columbia
V6P 6M9
Tel: (604) 323-7100
Fax: (604) 323-2600

1 3 5 7 9 10 8 6 4 2   03 02 01 00 99

Design by Frances Kay
Cover design by Jeannet Leendertse
Printed in the United States of America

CONTENTS

INTRODUCTION

For most of us, *counter-culture* conjures up images of a particular chapter of the American story. We associate it with the Beat movement and the sixties era, and with the infamous Summer of Love. The Free Speech movement, militant Yippies, and psychedelic drugs come to mind as well. All were symptomatic of the growing consensus among young people that the cultural mainstream was heading in the wrong direction.

Nowhere was this direction more apparent than in the San Francisco Bay Area, where Alan Watts was seen to be a spokesman for the movement. This was due in part to his Sunday-morning radio series *Way Beyond the West* (which aired on KPFA in Berkeley), and in part to his popular books on Zen Buddhism. By the late sixties, the City Lights edition of his pamphlet "Beat Zen, Square Zen, and Zen" had found its way into backpacks across the country, and many young people had come to consider him a sort of spiritual father to the hippies. Even his most outspoken critics would describe him as a "counter-cultural superstar," but those who understood his works realized that he held a far more encompassing view of the counter-culture—one with deep roots in Far Eastern culture and the mystical experience.

Born in England in 1915, Alan Watts became fascinated with stories about the Far East shortly after he began to read. He pored through popular adventure books about mysterious Chinese villains and discovered accounts of the enigmatic ways of Japanese samurai swordsmen and Zen masters. Following his self-pronounced fascination with "all things Oriental," he read every book he could find on the subject. By the early age of sixteen, he was speaking regularly at the Buddhist Lodge in London. It was there that Alan Watts met D. T. Suzuki and became acquainted with the yogic flavor of Hinduism and the Taoist influences of Zen Buddhism.

Years later he moved to New York, where he spent time with Joseph Campbell. In after-dinner conversation at the home of composer John Cage, they spoke about the Zen master's early tribal counterpart, the shamanic figures associated with peoples of Asia who, at their peak, inhabited most of the northern Pacific region, including areas of China, Japan, Siberia, and much of the Americas. As the conversation turned to the inward journeys and mystical experiences of the ancient shaman, it became apparent that shamanic ways continue into the present in the tradition of the living master, and that there have always been those who come to see the world in a manner dissociated from the mainstream way of thinking.

In the almost inconceivably ancient shamanic traditions, the artistic rock-art sites display elements of a thriving counterculture. The rituals of spiritual life were often observed in settings removed from daily activity. In the caves of France, the chambers where dancers sang and stomped before images of transcendent shaman figures and spirit animals are hidden deep within caverns that could only be accessed by crawling through narrow tunnels. In areas as far apart as Australia and southern California, the observance of solstice and other rites of renewal took place in caves large enough for only one or two people. As important as these ceremonies may have been, they were certainly not well attended.

From the earliest cave paintings, a consistency of style tells us that certain people painted the vivid rock-art images and wove sacred designs into baskets and blankets. Whether one considers ancient rock artists or more recent impressionist painters, these individuals have tended to separate themselves from the mainstream of social life and have focused their attentions on the creative life. The creative impulse that has entered society from these "outside" sources has often been regarded as a threat. But inevitably the diversity of perspective that comes out of these cultural experiments becomes vital to the culture, often in ways that could never have been predicted. Within each counter-culture lie the seeds of a new beginning. One might even look upon participants as the problem solvers who ultimately help the culture by introducing its next adaptive phase. With familiarity, as we have seen since the sixties, once-radical notions can become a part of daily life. Yoga, tai-chi, and all kinds of meditation were recently considered suspect, but today these arts are taught in shopping mall storefronts and make news in the corporate world as solutions to job-related stress.

Entire lifetimes have been spent exploring the ways in which intensely creative visionary impulses have influenced the cultures in which they occurred. Some of the philosophies that were of greatest interest to Alan Watts originated in India, China, and Japan as well as in Native America. In the modern West, we are now discovering East Indian influences through Buddhism, which in many ways simply presents the essential yogic practices of Hinduism with a greater psychological sophistication. In the method of Buddhism, Hinduism developed a strong social conscience, which is seen in the principle of the *bodhisattva,* who helps others along the path to enlightenment. In this sense, Buddhism reforms the Hindu view, integrating social concern with individual spiritual transformation.

At the same time, the Western separation of the experience of the divine from the role of the priest in the ancient Near East became the hallmark of what Joseph Campbell called the "religions of identity," so known for their emphasis on the individuals' identity *with* God instead of their experience *of* God. Predictably the history of the West has been full of rebellions of conscience against the spiritual tyranny of leaders who expected one to survive on a hand-me-down experience of the divine, or, as Alan Watts might have said, on a description of the meal instead of the meal itself. One finds here a clear view of the primary aspect of counter-culture: its basis in experience, particularly in the experience of the divine. Much of what follows is the inevitable impact this form of spiritual democracy will have upon art and, ultimately, on science.

The Culture of Counter-Culture is based on a series of Alan Watts's public lectures. They were selected for the insights they offer into how these elements have influenced our lives. This collection is far more than a review of the American psyche in the mid-1960s, for, through the words of Alan Watts, we discover what it was that made this revolution important and why its message will not be going away any time soon. These are not isolated revelations. They come from a tradition of diversity that is as old as culture itself, but they occurred at a rare time in modern history at which they are poised, once again, to influence the cultural mainstream in a meaningful way.

—Mark Watts
March 1998

MYSTICISM AND MORALITY

CHAPTER ONE

When I use the word *mysticism* I am referring to a kind of experience—a state of consciousness, shall we say—that seems to me to be as prevalent among human beings as measles. It is something that simply happens. And we don't know why it happens. All sorts of techniques claim to promote it and are more or less successful in doing so, but there is a peculiar thing that does happen to people. It is an experience that can actually be described from a number of quite different points of view, but we could add them up to a few dominant characteristics.

One ordinarily feels that one is a separate individual in confrontation with a world that is foreign to one's self, that is "not me." In the mystical kind of experience, though, that separate individual finds itself to be of one and the same nature or identity as the outside world. In other words, the individual suddenly no longer feels like a stranger in the world; rather, the external world feels as if it were his or her own body.

The next aspect of the mystical feeling is even more difficult to assimilate into our ordinary practical intelligence. It is the overwhelming sense that everything that happens—everything that I or anybody else has ever done—is part of a harmonious design and that there is no error at all.

Now, I am not talking about philosophy; I am not talking about a rationalization or some sort of theory that somebody cooked up in order to explain the world and make it seem a tolerable place in which to live. I am talking about a rather whimsical, unpredictable experience that suddenly hits people—an experience that includes this feeling of the total harmoniousness of everything.

I realize that those words—*the total harmoniousness of everything*—can carry with them a sort of sentimental or Pollyanna feeling. There are various religions in our society today that try to inculcate the belief that everything is harmonious unity. They want, in a sense, to propagandize the belief that everything is harmonious.

To my mind, that is a kind of pseudomysticism. It is an attempt to make the tail wag the dog or to make the effect produce the cause—because the authentic sensation of the true harmony of things is never brought about by insisting that everything is harmonious. When you do that—when you say to yourself, "All things are light, all things are God, all things are beautiful"—you are actually implying that they are not, because you wouldn't be saying it if you really knew it to be true.

So the sensation of universal harmony cannot come to us when it is sought or when we look for it as an escape from the way we actually feel or as compensation for the way we actually feel. It comes out of the blue. And when it does, it is overwhelmingly convincing. It is the foundation for most of mankind's profound philosophical, mystical, metaphysical, and religious ideas. Someone who has experienced this sort of thing cannot restrain himself. He has to get up and tell everybody about it. And, alas, he becomes the founder of a religion, because people say, "Look at that man, how happy he is, what conviction he has. He has no doubts. He seems so sure in everything he does."

This is the wonderful thing about a great human being. He is like an animal or a flower. When a flower bud opens, it has no hesitation or doubts. When a young woman appears in society as a debutante, she is not quite sure if she is going to come off. She appears on the stage of society with some doubts in her mind. And therefore all appearances of this kind are rather sickly in nature. But when the bird sings, or the chicken egg breaks or a flower buds, there is no doubt about it at all. It just comes forth.

And so, in the same way, when somebody has an authentic mystical experience, it just comes forth. He just has to tell everybody about it, because he notices everybody around him looking dreadfully serious. Looking as if they had a problem. Looking as if the act of living were extremely difficult. But from the standpoint of the person who has had this experience, they look funny. They don't understand that there isn't any problem at all.

The mystic has seen that the meaning of being alive is just to be alive. That is to say, when I look at the color of your hair and the shape of your eyebrow, I under-

3

stand that their shape and color are their point. And this is what we are all here for, as well: to be. It is so plain and so obvious and so simple. And yet, everybody rushes around in a great panic as if it were necessary to achieve something beyond themselves. The funny thing is, they are not even quite sure what they need to achieve, but they are devilishly intent on achieving it.

To the person who is in the state of consciousness I call mystical, this frenzy of activity all seems very weird, absurd. It is not to be criticized in an unkindly way, however. It's just a pity that they don't see their own absurdity.

One of the funny things about them is that they don't realize that there is a dimension, a sense in which their pursuit is magnificent. Jesus said, "Father, forgive them, for they know not what they do." I want to turn that into its opposite, in a way. I want to bless them—not forgive them—for not knowing what they're doing. I want to honor them, because the intensely serious preoccupations and anxieties of mankind appear to be not only absurd, but also a kind of marvel. They are a marvel in the same way, perhaps, that the protective coloring of a butterfly, which has somehow contrived to make its wings look like enormous eyes, is a marvel. When a bird that is about to devour it is confronted by these staring eyes, it hesitates a little, as you do when somebody stares at you. The butterfly appears to stare at the bird, and this phenomenon—the marvelous staring wings of the butterfly—seems to be a result of anxiety, the anxiety to survive all the problems and struggles of natural selection. And so, in our intense struggle, we are perhaps all unknowing poets.

One of the greatest ideas that has ever been produced is the Hindu idea that the world is a drama in which the central and supreme self behind all existence has gotten lost and has come to believe that it is not the one supreme self, but all the creatures that there are. It has come to believe in its own artistry. And the more involved, the more anxious, the more finite, the more limited the infinite manages to feel itself to be, the greater that artistry, the greater the depth of the illusion that it has created.

All art, in a way, is illusion. The art of the magician is the art of directing illusion, but all art, be it painting or theater, relies on illusions.

And so, the more anxiety there is, the more uncertainty there is, the more the universe has succeeded with its artistry. Just as when you are watching a play or reading a novel or viewing a movie, the more the author or actor manages to persuade you that the movie or novel is reality, the more he or she has succeeded as an artist. You may retain a faint recognition in the back of your mind that a play, for instance, is only a play. But when you are sitting on the edge of your seat and you are sweating and your hands are clutching the arms of the chair because the scene grips you, that play is magnificent art.

The Hindus feel that the whole arrangement of the cosmos is exactly like that: When in actual life you are wondering whether your doctor is a competent surgeon or a charlatan, or whether your investments are good or bad, the Hindus believe that all those feelings of crisis are exactly the same as the feelings you experience when you are sitting in the theater. As the Hindus would say, that thing in you that is real and that connects you under the surface with every other living being—that thing is the player of all the parts. It is the creator of the illusion. It is the source of the game that has got you so involved. And it is living it up in the same way the actors on the stage are living it up—and for the same reason: to convince you that the game is reality.

CHAPTER ONE

Everybody loves to play this game—the game of hide-and-seek, the game of scaring oneself with uncertainty. It is human. It is why we go to the theater or movies and why we read novels. And our so-called real life, seen from the position of the mystic, is a version of the same thing. The mystic is the person who has realized that the game is a game. It is hide-and-seek, and everything associated with the "hide" side of it is connected to those places within us where we as individuals feel lonely, impotent, put down, and so on—the negative side of existence.

I have tried at various times to show that there is really one simple principle that underlies everything: All insides have outsides. You don't know that the inside is an inside unless there is an outside. And you don't know that the outside is an outside unless there is an inside.

You—as you ordinarily experience yourself—are an inside. You are the animate, sensitive being inside your skin. But the inside of the skin goes with the outside of the skin. If there weren't an outside of the skin, there wouldn't be an inside. And the outside of the skin is the whole cosmos—galaxy after galaxy and everything else. And it goes with the inside in the same way that front goes with back. If you understand that, then you will truly feel the harmoniousness of everything. And that is the mystic's point of view.

Now, if I may switch subjects a little, what is morality?

Morality refers to a set of rules that are analogous to the rules of language. It is perfectly obvious that we can talk to each other in English, for instance, only if there is mutual agreement among ourselves as to how to use the language—what words refer to what experiences and how words are to be strung together so as to be useful and meaningful. It is interesting that we humans don't have much trouble in coming to this agreement about language. The police don't have to enforce grammar. The schoolteacher—yes—the schoolteacher sometimes has to enforce grammar with students and say in an authoritative way that they must use the correct grammatical forms. But when we grow up, we use these grammatical forms without much difficulty.

Just as we have to agree in order to communicate about language, we also have to agree about the rules of driving on the highway, the rules of doing business, the rules of banking, the rules of family arrangements, and so on. These rules are of the same kind as the rules of grammar. But, alas, this similarity is not often recognized, because the authority, the sanctions, the power behind these rules is different from the authority that underlies grammar. What I mean is this: If you transgress the rules of grammar, people just shrug their shoulders and say, "Well, he isn't making sense." They won't summon the police. But if you transgress the rules of the highway or of finances, someone is likely to call the cops. One senses the authority of the state behind those rules.

There are other rules that have behind them the authority of, not the state, but the Lord God Almighty. And if you transgress those rules, you are in danger not simply of going to jail, but, depending on your religious persuasion, of frying forever in hell. At the very least, you have shown yourself, lamentably, to be nothing better than a real person.

Now, wherever the domains of mysticism and morality come into conflict, there is a problem. Throughout the history of religion, mystics have always been suspect. Religions and their priests have been the upholders of moral rules. They have been the guardians of moral authority in the same way as lexicographers or grammarians have been the guardians of the rules of language. But when the mystical experience appears within the domain of religion, the priests always become very disturbed.

For example, recently in California there has been a strange outbreak within the Episcopal Church. Various congregations have experienced a phenomenon called *glossolalia*, which means "speaking in tongues."

If you turn on your radio on a Sunday night to any African-American revival meeting, you will hear glossolalia. The preacher begins by talking sensibly, but then, as the congregation gets more and more enthusiastic, saying, "Amen. Yes, Lord. Teach on that," the preacher works himself up to the point where he isn't talking sense anymore. He's just wailing, shouting, and celebrating the glorious nonsense of the universe.

In other words, all the dry, theological categories become poetry, as well as something beyond poetry: music. The preacher has become at that moment as one with the universe, because he is doing exactly what the stars are doing. The stars above and the galaxies are not making sense. They are just pouring out into the sky in a colossal display of fireworks.

Well, in recent months, various congregations of the Episcopal Church have had outbreaks of glossolalia. The Bishop of California, Bishop Pike, wrote an encyclical letter to his pastors that said, in effect, we must not be too dogmatic. We must recognize always that the spirit of God may work in mysterious ways that cannot be foreseen. We should keep an open mind about all these matters. This message was presented in a very complicated way, requiring several pages. But then, despite those sentiments, when it came to the question of the validity of speaking in tongues, the encyclical said, in no uncertain terms, *this must not happen in the*

Episcopal Church. There was an iron hand in Bishop Pike's velvet glove.

This has been the characteristic attitude of priests and guardians of law and order throughout the ages. Everything, as they say in the Episcopal Church, should be done decently and in order.

The guardians of this kind of law and order have always been afraid of the spontaneous manifestations of the spirit. Not simply of things like mysticism, but also of things like falling in love. This leads to an absolutely astounding paradox. We know that human love is genuine only when it is felt in the depth of the heart. And we know that this is true whether it be love for another human or love of God. And, of course, we are always looking to receive genuine love. We don't want others to love us because they are forced to. We want them to love us because they really do love us in their hearts.

When you study the history of the Hebrews, which underlies Christianity, you will discover two traditions constantly compensating for one another and playing off each other: the priestly tradition and the prophetic tradition. The priesthood is concerned with the external observance of laws. The prophetic tradition is concerned with the internal motivations behind actions. Prophets constantly condemn the meaningless adherence to law as hypocritical. In this sense, Jesus is the greatest of the prophets. Even if a man has never committed adultery, the prophet says that if he has looked at a woman with lust, he has already committed adultery in his heart. To really obey the law, in other words, you must obey it with your feelings and not just outwardly. For as Jeremiah says, "The day will come when no man shall any more say to his brother, 'Know God'—that is to say, 'know the law of God'—but they shall all know me, for I will write my law in their inward parts."

The ideal, in other words, is the person who does not simply obey the rules, but whose desires are transformed from the heart. To have the law written on the heart means to change one's desire.

And this peculiarly paradoxical situation exists within the established church: being required or forced by law to be loving, while at the same time being required to feel that love in one's heart.

This is where the astonishing conflict between the mystic and moralist occurs. For the mystic knows that he has to be more than the legalist. He has to do more than outwardly observe the law. Luther said that the law that requires inward compliance is the most terrible thing. A great deal of his philosophy was an attack on the idea that one's inner feelings could be commanded, because the moment you subscribe to the idea that your inner feelings should be commanded, you open the door to hypocrisy. If you tell others that you love them simply because you know you are supposed to love them, but in your heart, you don't love them at all, then you are a liar and a hypocrite. And the more you insist on that lie— and the more you feel it is your duty to change your feelings and love others—the deeper and deeper you get into trouble. The truth will come out. You will not be able to sustain the pretense. You will not have sufficient energy to go on pretending and making a mockery of the feeling of love. And, if you are honest, you will have to say at last, "I don't love." It doesn't matter whether you have to say this to some other human being or, in a religious situation, if you have to sit back and say to the Lord, "Lord, I don't love you. I think you are a bore. You are demanding. You are authoritarian. You are domineering. I probably ought to love you, but I don't."

Now, we are afraid that an honest expression of our feelings would be disruptive to law and order. But it wouldn't. Not in the least. Actually it would contribute to law and order.

I was once associated in a business way with somebody who was a complicated person. He always pretended that he was a great idealist and that whatever he was doing was for the benefit of mankind, for the furtherance of mutual understanding, and to promote unselfishness and love between human beings. Actually, his dealings were very shady ethically. And I couldn't get along with him, because he wouldn't come clean. If he had said, "Look, I'm in a jam, and in order to get around it, I need you to manipulate things with me thus and so. I know this isn't ethical, but this is what I need you to do." I would have said, "Well, I'm entirely in agreement with you." If he hadn't come on in his usual pious way, which I found sickening and offensive, but had come on in a human way, we would have understood each other.

This example shows that real honesty is a genuine basis for morality. Real honesty means not pretending that your feelings are other than they are. Sometimes we may have to do things that go against our feelings. For example, you may have to help people whom you don't like and you don't want to help. Don't be dishonest. Don't say that your feelings are different from what they are.

Now we can perhaps understand something about the deep relationship between morals and mysticism. If we go back to the mystical experience that I described earlier in terms of the harmoniousness of everything, we can see that such harmony applies to human behavior, too. Its ups and downs are no different in principle from the behavior of the clouds or the wind or dancing flames in a fireplace.

When you watch the pattern of the dancing

flames, you see that they never do anything vulgar. Their artistry is always perfect.

Ultimately, it is the same with human beings. We are just as much a part of the natural order as flames in the fire or stars in the sky. But this is only apparent to the person who is honest, in the sense in which I have been using that word. The person who is tied up with trying to pretend that his feelings are other than what they actually are can never see this. He will always be a troublemaker. He is the original hypocrite. The one who is most destructive is the person who pretends to be a model of love and rectitude and justice, when in fact he isn't. And nobody really can be. Altogether superior to the hypocrite is the person I call the loving cynic, who knows of course that everybody has weaknesses, but who isn't contemptuous of anyone for that reason.

A book that illuminates the mind of a loving cynic is *Memories, Dreams and Reflections*, by C. G. Jung. It is the autobiography of a man who was a superb human being, in the particular sense of thoroughly knowing his own limitations and having a sense of humor about it. Jung was a man who understood how to integrate into his being the devilish and compulsive aspects of his nature.

In the metaphysical sphere, the mystic is the one who feels that everything that happens is in some way right, is in some way an integral, harmonious part of the universe. Now, when we transplant or translate that idea into the moral sphere, the sphere of human conduct, the equivalent insight is this: There are no wrong feelings. There may be wrong actions, in the sense of actions contrary to the rules of human behavior. But the way you feel towards other people—loving them, hating them, and so on—is never wrong. And it's absurd and dishonest to try and force your feelings to be other than they are.

The idea that there are no wrong feelings is immensely threatening to people who are afraid to feel. This is one of the peculiar problems of Western culture: We are terrified of our feelings, because they take off on their own. We think that if we give them any scope, if we don't immediately beat them down, they will lead us into all kinds of chaotic and destructive actions.

It is funny that we in our Western culture today believe this—we who do more chaotic and reckless things than any culture has ever done before. If, instead, we would accept our feelings and look upon their comings and goings as something that is as beautiful and as natural and as necessary as changes in the weather or the sequence of night and day or the four seasons, we would be at peace with ourselves. Because what has been problematic for Western man is not so much his struggles with other people and their needs and problems, but rather his struggles with his own feelings—with what he will allow himself to feel and what he won't allow himself to feel. He is ashamed to feel profoundly sad. It is unmanly to cry. He is ashamed to loathe somebody, because he has been told not to hate people. He is ashamed to be overcome with the beauty of something—whether a natural landscape or a member of the opposite sex—because being overcome means not being in control. As a result of this repression, he ends up going out of his mind. We are always out of control when we don't accept our feelings, when we try to pretend that our inner life is different from what it really is.

The most releasing thing that anybody can possibly understand is that our inner feelings are never wrong. They may not be a correct guide to how we should act, of course. If you feel that you hate someone intensely, it isn't necessarily right to go up to that person and cut his throat. But it is right that you should have the feeling of hate. For you see, when a person comes to himself, he comes to be one with his own feelings. And that is the only way to control them.

The sailor always keeps the wind in his sail. Whether he wants to sail with the wind or against it, he always uses the wind. He never denies the wind.

In the same way, a person has to keep in contact with his own feelings. Whether he wants to act as his feelings obviously suggest or in a different way, he still has to keep his feelings with him, because they are his own essential self. As soon as he abandons his feelings, he has lost himself. He becomes an empty mask with no real life behind it. And all his protestations of love and goodwill will be hollow.

If a woman has a child conceived by accident, she may think, "I really didn't want to have this baby, and I don't want the responsibility, but I mustn't think those thoughts. All good mothers love their babies." And so she says to her child, "I love you." But her milk is sour, and the baby becomes confused.

It would be much better if the mother said to the baby, "Listen, you are a pest and a nuisance, and I didn't want you." Then they would understand each other. Everything would be clear. There would be no confusions, and no one would feel mixed up. And because when you feel that somebody is a pest and a nuisance, and you tell him so, you are apt, after awhile, to develop a kind of humorous feeling about your irritation with him. After awhile, you might even start saying, "You old bastard" with a kind of affection. The point is that, through their honesty, both the adult and child keep in touch with their true feelings, and instead of denying a difficult situation, they face it, and may in fact grow out of it.

So, what the mystic feels while in the mystical state of mind is the divinity, the glory, of everything that is.

And when we apply that mystical insight to the moral sphere, it is one's genuine feelings that are divine and glorious. Therefore, these genuine feelings must always be admitted, must always be allowed. Let me emphasize once more that this doesn't mean that we are therefore always compelled to act upon our feelings—to kill the person we hate, for instance. On the contrary, conscious hatred need not lead to violence at all. In fact, it is most often unconscious hatred that leads to violence. What I am saying is that it is the recognition and acceptance of what one honestly feels that is the moral equivalent of the mystic's vision of the divinity of existence.

CHAPTER TWO

B etween the realm of Western psychology, psychiatry, and psychotherapy and the realm of
the so-called religions of Asia, there is common ground because both are interested in
changing states of human consciousness. However, the
Near Eastern religions that have become institutions in
the West—including Christianity, Judaism, and even
Islam—are relatively less interested in this matter.
Western religions are more concerned with behavior,
doctrine, and belief than with any transformation of the
way in which we are aware of ourselves and the world.
This matter concerns psychiatry and psychology very
deeply. However, those states of consciousness that are

not normal are usually treated in Western psychology as sick.

There are, of course, exceptions to this rule. In the work of Jung, Grodock, Princehorn, and more modern psychologists such as Rogers and Laing, changing consciousness is often looked upon as a form of therapy. But in general, a state of consciousness different from the normal is regarded as a form of sickness. Therefore, institutional psychiatry constitutes itself as the guardian of sanity and the socially approved experience of reality. Very often reality seems to be as it is seen on a bleak Monday morning, and this has become the official doctrine—I might even say dogma—of what reality is. After all, we know that our science is founded in the scientific naturalism of the nineteenth century, and the metaphysical and mythological assumptions of that science still underlie a great deal of psychological thinking. In behaviorism particularly, but also in official psychoanalysis, we see the emphasis placed on the scientific model.

Indeed, one might say that psychoanalysis is based on Newtonian mechanics, and could be called psychohydraulics. There are certainly respects in which our psychic life exhibits the dynamics of water, but of course we want to know how reliable the model is. For the scientific naturalism of the nineteenth century, the basic energies of nature were considered to be very much inferior to human consciousness in quality. The biologist of that time would think of the energy of the universe as blind energy. Correspondingly, it seems to me that Freud thought of the libido as essentially uncaring, unconscious energy embodying only a kind of formless, unstructured, and insatiable lust.

This tendency to regard all that lies below the surface of human consciousness as being less evolved was influenced by the contemporary thinking in the field of biology: namely, Darwin's theory of evolution, of seeing the human mind as a fortuitous development from more primitive forms of life. This development occurred by purely mechanical processes, by natural selection, and by the survival of the fittest.

In general, man was seen as a fluke of nature and as an embodiment of reason, emotion, and values for which the more basic processes of nature had no sympathy and about which they did not care. If, therefore, the human race was to flourish, we had to take charge of evolution. It should no longer be left to spontaneous processes, but must be directed by human ingenuity. Now, this presents an interesting problem, since most people cannot consider more than three variables at the same time without using a pencil. This inability shows that in many ways the scanning process of man's conscious attention is quite inadequate for dealing with the infinitely varied, multidimensional processes of the natural universe. A serious attempt has been made to control these processes, and scientific naturalism places man in a fantastic fight with nature.

This whole notion of the conquest and subordination of nature has ancient, nonscientific origins. The idea of man as the head and ruler of nature is in the Western image of God and has become a rationale for human dominance. Yet the time has dawned when our attempts to beat nature into submission are having alarming results. We see that it is very dangerous to mess around with processes that we don't understand, that have enormous numbers of variables, and we have begun to wonder whether we hadn't better leave well enough alone.

Now, although I said Western psychology had more interests in common with Oriental religion than it does with Western religion, there is a sense in which psychiatry and psychotherapy are, in effect, becoming the religion of the West. Psychoanalysis has much in common with the forms and procedures of institutional religion. For example, there is in psychoanalysis, as there is in Christianity, apostolic succession: the passing down of qualified power to practice therapy from the father/founder Sigmund Freud through his immediate apostles to an enormous company of archbishops and bishops. Within this group, there are heresiarchs such as Jung, Grodock, Rank, and Reich, and the heresiarchs are duly excommunicated and anathematized. There are rituals in psychoanalysis, as there are with religion. There is the sacrament of the couch and the spiritual discipline of free association. There is the mystic knowledge of the interpretation of dreams, and there are also the two great symbolic fetishes: the long one and the round one.

It is extraordinarily easy to make fun of all this. However, we must not forget that we owe a tremendous debt to Freud for pointing out that much of ourselves—of which we are aware in terms of the conscious ego—is not really ourselves. It is something superficial, and however we define its nature, the realities of human life are not under the gaze of its scanning process, at least not in the ordinary way. That was a tremendous revelation. But one sees troublesome signs when the doctrines and processes of psychiatry, psychoanalysis, and so forth become officialized. Thomas Szasz, in his books *The Myth of Mental Illness* and *The Manufacture of Madness*, points out something extremely important to us: The psychological official of today has become the priest. He is beginning to exercise the same sort of controls over human life as were exercised by the church in the Middle Ages. A professor of psychiatry at Columbia or Harvard or Yale medical schools today has the same sort of intellectual respectability and authority as the professor of theology at the University of Toledo or Padua would have had in the year 1400.

Now you must realize that the theologians of those days believed completely in their cosmology and theology, in the same way that our scientists know certain things to be true today—despite the fact that they change their opinions very often while they hold them. Their ideas have the force of dogma, as witness the anathematization of Velikowsky for his uncomfortable ideas. There are heresies today that are persecuted in the same way as heresies were persecuted by the Inquisition. They are persecuted out of kindness in exactly the same way that the Inquisition persecuted heresy out of kindness and deep concern for human beings.

It is hard for us today to understand that form of kindness. But if you seriously believe that someone who voluntarily rejects the Catholic faith will be physically and spiritually tortured forever in hell, you would resort to almost any means to save that person from such a fate—especially if the disease of heresy from which he suffers is infectious.

You might first try to reason with him. If he did not respond to reason, you might resort to abuse and forceful argument. If he was still unresponsive, you might give him shock treatment and bang him about. If that didn't work, you might try the thumb screw, the rack, and the iron maiden. And if that didn't work—as a last desperate attempt—you might burn him at the stake in the pious hope that in the midst of those searing fires he would think better and make a last act of perfect contrition and so be rescued from everlasting damnation. You would do all this believing "this is going to hurt me more than it's going to hurt you" and in the spirit of the surgeon who is very sorry indeed that he has to make you undergo this extremely painful operation, but it is in your best interest, and there really is at least a fifty-fifty chance that you will survive.

Likewise, in the name of science and medicine, people may be deprived of their civil rights arbitrarily and without due process, incarcerated in institutions that are often worse than prisons, and generally left to rot. They may be neglected and ignored. Or when they are bumptious, they may be given shock treatment or put in solitary confinement. And for what? Because they have unorthodox and heretical states of consciousness.

Most of these people are not dangerous until provoked by being ignored by being treated as nonhuman. Now, if you are labeled nonhuman, there is little you can do about it, because everything you say that sounds human will be taken as an utterance of a mechanical man imitating humanness out of lunatic cunning. You will be treated with suspicion, and everything you say will be listened to with different ears. And you will have one heck of a time talking your way out of it, because there really are no rules as to what one must do to escape being incarcerated for having unorthodox consciousness. There is no clear road to repentance.

Likewise, in jails where people are serving one- to ten-year sentences, there is a desperate feeling that there is no way out. I have visited prisons in places like Vacaville, California. There, young men have come to me in perfect desperation and said, "I don't know what's happened to me. I want to live like a decent citizen. I know I've done things that are wrong, but I simply don't know what is expected of me here. If I try to do what's expected, they say I'm compliant, and that seems to be some sort of a sickness."

Thomas Szasz drew attention to this when he quoted a discussion of the types of schoolchildren who may need therapy. There were both overachieving and underachieving children. There were children who exhibited erratic patterns and those who were dully mediocre. In fact, the behavior of every sort of child can be given a diagnostic name that sounds sick. As Jung once said, "Life itself is a disease with a very poor prognosis. It lingers on for years and invariably ends with death."

I submit that with our present knowledge of the human mind, placing power in the hands of psychiatrists is amazingly dangerous. I would suggest that today we know about as much concerning the human mind as we knew about the galaxy in 1300. While there are indeed individuals who are able to perform psychotherapy, it is the sheerest arrogance for anybody to say that he is officially qualified to do so. We do not know how psychotherapy is done, just as we do not really know how musical, artistic, and literary genius is accomplished. You can put the tools for doing these things in people's hands, and you can show them how to use the tools, but whether they will use those tools with genius is unpredictable.

This is true of the art of psychotherapy. You cannot really teach it, and we don't know how it's done. We have only vague ideas. Probably there are some people who, by reason of their mental state, are not qualified to perform psychotherapy because they intend to derange other people. But to say that there are certain standards and examinations that can be passed and certificates that can be issued that qualify people for this work is pernicious nonsense. Qualifications are used by those who consider themselves official therapists out of economic self-interest. It is a way to disable their competition.

The same kind of self-interest is seen in religion. Some years ago, I was looking at some books in a bookshop in Thailand. I noticed a book on a certain form of Buddhist meditation, and I murmured, "Hmm,

Satipatthana," which is the name of a certain kind of Buddhist meditation.

A voice suddenly said, "You practice Satipatthana?" I looked up and there was a skinny Buddhist monk in a yellow robe with rather red eyes looking at me.

I said, "Not exactly Satipatthana. I use a different method. It's called Zen."

"Oh Satipatthana not Zen."

I said, "Well, it's something like it, isn't it?"

"No."

"Well, it's rather like yoga," I said. "Isn't it?"

"Not yoga, no. Satipatthana different. Only right way."

"Well, look," I said to him. "I have a lot of Roman Catholic friends who tell me that their way is the only right way. Whom am I to believe? You know, you're like someone who's got a ferryboat for crossing the river, and another fellow down the stream has opened up a ferry business. You go to the government, and say, 'He's not authorized to operate a ferryboat,' because he's your competition. On the contrary, let all operate ferryboats who will. And if you haven't got the sense to get off one that sinks, it's your fault."

It's interesting that official psychiatry has curious things in common with Western religion as well as with Eastern philosophies. It is like Eastern thought insofar as it has an interest in states of consciousness, although it is inclined to regard states of consciousness other than the ordinary as sick. But it has one very important feature in common with Western religion as well, and to understand that we have to go a little bit deeper into Western religious history and ask ourselves what in Western religion—especially in Christianity, but also in Judaism—is the great heresy?

Curiously enough the great heresy was first committed by no less a person than Jesus Christ who believed himself to be God. This fact is unquestionably true if you think that the Gospel of St. John has historical value. This issue is a little more vague in the synoptic Gospels, but if you read the Gospel of St. John there is absolutely no doubt about it. Jesus said, "I and the Father are one. He who has seen me has seen the Father. Before Abraham was, I am. I am the way, the truth, and the light. I am the resurrection and the life." He said all that, according to this Gospel, and that is something that in the Western world you are not supposed to say. And even more importantly, you are not supposed to believe it, and naturally that was very difficult for Jesus because he was saying all this in the context of the Hebrew culture. He tried to find language in the Hebrew scriptures with which to express his state of consciousness. He had an unusual state of consciousness that I would call cosmic consciousness. This is otherwise known as mystical experience, and it is also known in the Far East as *moksha*, *nirvana*, *bodhi*, and *satori*.

Call it what you will, this awakening happens to people, and it has happened as far back as we know. It happens in cultures all over the world, and we don't know very much about it. We don't really know how to make it happen because it seems to come as a spontaneous surprise. But it unquestionably happens, and most people keep their mouths shut about it when it does.

I had a friend who, in the middle of having a stroke, had an illumination. Afterward, he said to me, "I fear to speak to my friends of this, but it was the most beautiful experience. I shall never be afraid of death. In fact, I recommend a stroke to everyone." This was my friend Jean Varda, the lately deceased Greek painter.

Jesus certainly had this transformation of consciousness, and he was crucified for it because he committed an act of insubordination and treason against the cosmic government as it was popularly understood at that time. For if you believe that God is an absolute, omniscient, and omnipotent authority—a sort of cosmic ego—then to claim to hold that same power is to introduce democracy into the Kingdom of Heaven. To do so is to usurp divine authority and to speak in its name without proper authorization. The disciples asked Jesus, "By what authority do you speak—of heaven or of men?" Jesus was tricky and said, "By what authority did John the Baptist speak?" They were a bit nervous about answering that one. He could have asked by what authority did Isaiah speak, or Moses?

Of course Moses became official authority, and if you could wangle it, you said that your words were simply an extension of what Moses said, because Rabbi So-and-so said it who got it from Rabbi So-and-so who got it from Rabbi So-and-so who got it from Moses. If you said that, then it was okay.

Notice that to be an authority today in the academic world depends on documentation. It is not enough to say, "For I say unto you." You must put in your footnotes, and the more the footnotes, the greater your authority. So our dissertations tend to be books about books about books, and our libraries multiply by mitosis.

But when somebody speaks as an authority, that really means to speak as an *author*. It means that this is a statement of which you are the author and, therefore, for which you assume responsibility. So to speak with authority is to be original—not to be aberrant—but to speak from the origin. That is what Christians mean when they say to speak in the spirit. It is to have your mouth possessed by the Holy Spirit, as they believe the mouth of Jesus was possessed by the Holy Spirit.

So the Gospel of Jesus, which of course was hushed up from its inception, was simply, "Wake up, everybody, and find out who you are!" Again in the

Gospel of St. John, Jesus—pointing to his disciples—said they, too, may be one, "even as you, Father, and I, are one." So when he was accused of blasphemy and the Jews took up stones to stone him, he said, "Many good works have I shown you from the Father, and for which of these do you stone me?" And they said, "For a good work we do not stone you but for blasphemy, because you, being a man, make yourself God." Now listen to the reply. He said, "Is it not written in your law, 'I have said ye are Gods'? And if that is what the Scripture says, it cannot be denied. So why do you tell me that I blaspheme because I say, 'I am a Son of God'?" And of course there was no answer.

It doesn't say that in your King James translation of the Bible: *I am a Son of God*. Instead, it says, *I am* the *Son of God*. You will see the italicized text, and you might think that is done for emphasis if you don't realize that passages in italics in the King James Bible are interpolations by the translators. In Greek, leaving out the definite article is equivalent to using the indefinite article. So "Son of" in Hebrew and Arabic means "of the nature of." When we call someone a "son of a bitch," we mean bitchy. And so if you call someone a "Son of God," you mean divine or of the nature of God. As the Nicene Creed subsequently defined it, "He is of one substance with the Father."

Jesus' words were blasphemy for the Jews, and so they became blasphemy for the Christians. It was simply not all right for anyone other than Jesus to say this. They said, "Okay. It was so with you, but there it stops! There will be no more of this." And as a result of that distinction, Jesus was made irrelevant by pedestalization. He was kicked upstairs, in spite of the fact that he said, "Greater works than these that I do, shall you do." It was upstairs for him, because we just cannot have that sort of thing going on in a monarchical universe. We're not going to have democracy in the Kingdom of Heaven. So this is why the Gospel is impossible, because we are supposed to follow the example of Christ when he says, "Be not anxious for the morrow." Do not worry about what you shall eat, what you shall drink, and what you shall wear. God will take care of you. Doesn't he take care of the birds? Don't the flowers grow in their crazy, wonderful way? This is great, so what are you worrying about? But I have never heard a sermon on this passage, because it's totally subversive. If people followed it, the economy would collapse.

So instead religious leaders have said, "Oh yes, that's all very well, but he was the boss' son." He had that colossal advantage, so take up your cross and follow him.

But wait a minute! We don't know if we are going to be resurrected three days later, and we can't perform all those miracles. He had an unfair advantage, so how can they ask us to follow the example of Christ?

On the other hand, suppose he meant what he said, and he didn't have an unfair advantage. Suppose that what was true for Jesus as the Son of God is true for us. Only a few of us know it, and we are careful to be quiet about it lest the same thing happen to us as happened to Jesus—as indeed it often does.

Occasionally someone from the Bible Belt—who never heard of the *Upanishads*—has this cosmic consciousness experience. He realizes that that's what happened to Jesus, and he says, "I'm Jesus too." Well, everybody says to him, "You aren't Jesus. It's pretty obvious you're not Jesus. You're just Joe Nobody." To which he might reply, "Well, that's what they said about Jesus." He has a perfect argument, except they are apt to say, "If you're Jesus, turn these stones into bread." And he might as well reply, "A wicked and deceitful genera-tion seeketh for a sign, and there shall be no sign given."

Now, why is this significant? Is it important for the human being to realize that in some sense of the word—whatever it means—he is God or one with God, as is plainly taught by the Hindus and hinted at by the Buddhists? Notice that the Buddhists don't like to express this realization as a concept because people tend to use the concept as an idol to hang onto. The Buddhists want you to find out for yourself—and not simply believe in it. And certainly the Taoists understand it, and the Sufis understand it. A lot of people under-stand it. But so what?

The importance of this recognition is this: To know that you are God is another way of saying that you feel completely with this universe. You feel pro-foundly rooted in it and connected with it. You feel, in other words, that the whole energy that expresses itself in the galaxies—whatever that is—is intimate. It is not something to which you are a stranger. It is that with which you are intimately bound—in your seeing, your hearing, your talking, your thinking, and your moving. In all of this, you express that which moves the sun and other stars.

If you don't know that you are God, you feel alien. You feel like a stranger in the world. And if you feel like a stranger, you become hostile. You might start to bull-doze the world about and try to make it submit to your will. Ecologically, you become a real troublemaker.

Another reason you might become hostile is that you may have the feeling that you were just brought into this place, that your father and mother were up to some monkey business, and you didn't ask to be here. If you feel this way, you always feel you can turn around and blame them. You can always blame somebody. You can blame the government. You can blame the rascals. You can blame the cheaters. Of course, to blame others you must suppose that you yourself aren't a rascal of some sort, and what are the chances of that?

But you can always blame someone and say, "I didn't ask for it. Take it away." And yet, very few people are really ready to take it away.

Camus once said, "The only serious philosophical problem is whether or not to commit suicide." If you choose *not* to commit suicide, what are you going to do? Now you have made the decision to live, and you must assume responsibility for it. You have to say "yes" to what happens. It is your *karma*.

There are many popular misinterpretations of the doctrine of karma. It is usually understood to be that what happens to you, either fortunate or unfortunate, is the result of good or bad deeds in a previous life or at a previous time in this life. But that is popular superstition. In Sanskrit, karma means simply "doing." And if I say that something "is your karma," I am saying "it is your doing." So a book that expounds karma would be not so much a *whodunit* as a *youdunit*. But that seems fantastic to us because we are still uncomfortable with the idea that we are the works, all that there is.

WHAT IS REALITY?

CHAPTER THREE

I wonder if it has ever occurred to you how really curious it is that we regard almost everything we experience as something that happens to *us*, as something not originated by us, but as the expression of a power or an activity that is external to us. Now, if we consider the implications of this, we realize that what we mean by our *self* is narrowly circumscribed. Even events that go on inside our own bodies are put in the same category as actions that happen outside our skins. A thunderstorm or an earthquake, for instance, just happens to us—we are obviously not responsible for them. In the same way, we think that hiccups just happen to us, too, and belly rumbles just happen to us. We are not responsible for them. And as for the catastrophic fact of our being born, well, we had nothing to do with that, either. And so we can spend all our life blaming our parents for putting us in the situations in which we find ourselves.

This way of looking at the world—in a sort of passive mood—permeates our general feeling about life. As Westerners, we are accustomed to looking at human existence as a precarious event occurring within a cosmos that, on the whole, is completely unsympathetic and alien to our existence. We have been reared within an early twentieth-century form of common sense, based on the philosophy of the science of the nineteenth century, which rejected Christianity and Judaism. Therefore, we tend to regard ourselves as biological accidents in a stupid and mechanical universe that has no finer feelings and that is nothing more than a vast, pointless gyration of radioactive rocks and gas.

Alternatively—if we have a more traditional outlook—we see ourselves as children of God and, therefore, under God's authority. We believe that there is a big boss on top of the universe who has allowed us, at his pleasure, to have the disgusting effrontery to exist. So we'd better mind our Ps and Qs, because that boss is always ready to punish us, with the attitude of "this is going to hurt me more than it is going to hurt you."

When we adopt either of these world views—the scientific or traditional—then we are defining the world as something to which we do not really belong. We are not really part of it. I would use a stronger word than *part*, except that we do not have such a word in English. I'd have to say something like *connected with* or *essential to*.

It is quite alien to Western thought to conceive that the external world—which is defined as something that happens to us—and our bodies are *us*, because we have a myopic view of what we are. It is as if we have arbitrarily limited how much of ourselves we regard as us. It is as if we have focused our attention on certain restricted areas of the whole panorama of things that we are and have said, "I will accept only so much of me, and I will take sides against the rest."

This leads us to an extremely important principle, which can be illustrated by the fact that we see the same thing in different ways when we view it at different levels of magnification. That is to say, when we look at something with a microscope, we see it in a certain way, and when we look at the same thing with the naked eye, we see it differently, and when we look at it with a telescope, we see it in yet another way.

Which level of magnification is correct? Obviously, they are all correct. They are just different points of view. When you look at a newspaper photograph, you may see a human face. Look at that face with a magnifying glass, though, and you will see nothing but a profusion of dots, scattered meaninglessly. Move away from those dots—which seem to be separate from each other—and once again they will suddenly arrange themselves into a pattern. Those individual dots add up to something that makes sense.

Likewise, if we take a myopic view of ourselves— as most of us do—we may overlook some larger sense of us that is not apparent to us in our ordinary, myopic consciousness.

When we examine our bloodstreams under a microscope, we see that there is one hell of a fight going on. All sorts of microorganisms are chewing each other up. And if we became overly fascinated by our view of our own bloodstream as seen in the microscope, we might start taking sides in that battle, which would be fatal to us. The health of our organism depends on the continuance of this battle. In other words, what seems like conflict at one level of magnification is actually harmony at a higher level.

Considering this, could it possibly be that we—with all our problems, conflicts, neuroses, sicknesses, political outrages, wars, and tortures—are actually in a state of harmony? Well, it is claimed that some human beings have in fact broken through to exactly that vision. Somehow or other they have slipped into a state of consciousness in which they can see the apparent disintegration and disorganization of everyday life as the completely harmonious functioning of a larger totality.

This insight depends on overcoming the illusion that space separates things. That is to say, your body and mine, our births and deaths, and the births of others after our deaths are events with intervals between them. Normally we regard those intervals in time and space as having no importance, no function. We tend to think that the universe consists primarily of stars and galaxies. They are what we notice. The space containing them is sort of written off, as if it weren't really there.

What one has to realize, though, is that space is an essential function of the things that are in it. After all, you can't have separate stars unless there is space separating them. Eliminate the space, and there will be no stars at all. And vice versa. There could be no space in any meaningful sense whatsoever if there weren't physical bodies in it. So that the bodies in space and the space surrounding them are two aspects of a single continuum. They are related in exactly the same way a back and a front are related. You just cannot have one without the other. The moment you realize that intervals in space and time are connective, you will understand that you cannot be defined exclusively as a flash of consciousness occurring between two eternal darknesses. That is the current, common-sense point of view that we Westerners have of our own lives. We consider that in the darkness that comes before our birth, we were nothing, and in the eternal darkness that will follow our death, we likewise will be nothing.

I am going to discuss these matters—not by appealing to any special, spooky knowledge, as if I've been traveling on a higher plane and remember all my previous incarnations and can therefore tell you authoritatively that you are much more than just your isolated individuality. I am going to base my discussion on common sense and facts that everybody has access to.

First of all, you have to realize that life is a pattern of immense complexity. What is the body, for instance? The body is something that is recognizable. You recognize your friends when you meet them. Although every time you see them, they are absolutely different from what they were. They are not constant, just as the flame of a candle is not constant.

We know that a candle flame is a stream of hot gas, but still we say "the flame of the candle" as if it were a constant. And we do that because the flame has a constant, recognizable pattern. The spear-shaped outline of the flame and its coloration form a constant pattern. And in exactly the same way, we are all constant patterns. And that is all we are. The only constant thing about us is our *doing*—the way we dance—rather than our being. Except that there is no *I* that dances. There is just the dancing, just as the flame is the streaming of hot gas. And just as a whirlpool in a river is a whirling of water. There is no whirlpool. There is only a thing that whirlpools. And in the same way, each one of us is a very delightfully complex undulation of the energy of the whole universe. Only by process of miseducation have we been deprived of that knowledge.

Not that there is someone to blame for this,

because such miseducation is always done with our own tacit consent. Life is basically a game of hide-and-seek. Life is a pulse—on and off. Here it is, and now it isn't. And by means of this pulsation, we know life is there. Just as we know what we mean by on because we know what we mean by off. That is why, when we want to awaken someone, we knock at the door. We keep up a knocking pulsation, because that on-ness and off-ness attracts attention.

All life is this flickering on and off. And there are many different rhythms to it. There are fast flickerings, like the reaction of light upon our eyes. If we take a lighted cigarette and move it, in the dark, in a circle, we will see a circle in the air, because the image of that cigarette on our retina lasts. It endures in the same way that an image stays on a radar screen until it is revivified by another sweep of the radar antenna.

Your eye notices continuity between separate events. Very fast impulses are perceived as constant forms. We see fast impulses as solid things. When the blades of a propeller or an electric fan are turning, the separate blades become a solid disk and you cannot throw an egg through it. In the same way, you can't put your finger through a rock, even though it's mostly empty space. The atoms in it are moving too fast. That is the meaning of the whole phenomenon of hardness. Hardness in nature is immense energy acting in a very concentrated, restricted space, and that is why you can't push your finger through something that's hard.

Along with these very tiny and fast rhythms—which give us the impression of continuity—there are also in this universe immensely slow rhythms. And these are very difficult for us to keep track of. One very slow rhythm impresses us and depresses us as being our own life and death, our own coming and going. This rhythm moves at such a slow pace that we can't possibly believe that it is really a rhythm at all. We think of our birth as something quite unique that could never occur again. But that's only because we are so close to it, you see, and because the on-and-off pulse of our life is so slow.

From that point of view, we are, as Marshall McLuhan said, "driving a car while looking at the rear-view mirror." This means that the environment in which we believe our self to exist is always a past environment. It isn't the one we are actually in.

The process of growth, which is the basic process of biology, is one in which lower orders are always being superseded by higher orders. The lower order can never—or rarely—figure out the nature of the higher order that is taking over. Therefore, the lower orders may see the higher orders as terrible threats, as total disasters, as the end of the world. We can never really know what the next step is going to be. If we did, we couldn't take it, because it would already be past. Any known future event is one of which we can say, "We've already had it." In that sense, it is past.

When we play a game such as chess, and the outcome of the game becomes certain, we stop the game and begin a new one. Because the whole zest of the thing lies in not knowing the future. The whole universe is a game of hide-and-seek. The point of that game as it is understood by the Hindus is that we don't know what the next order is going to be. But we can be sure that it will be an order of some kind, and it will comprehend us.

We are currently at a moment in history that we view as the beginning of a great countdown to the end of the human race. In this atomic age, we face the terrifying possibility that we may obliterate our planet and turn the whole globe into a cinder.

Imagine that you know exactly when the end of the world is coming. You count down to the final explosion. Seven, six, five, four, three, two, one. Suddenly there's a great roar, and you recognize it. Where have you heard it before? On the seashore, that's where, listening to the waves coming in and going out.

We don't stop to think that we are waves, too, coming in and going out. But that is what everything in the universe is. And when one wave mounts and mounts and gets too big for its boots, it spills and breaks. And we are like that. It is very important to realize that sometimes we are a crashing wave, so that then we won't panic when it happens. The person who presses the button that ends the world will be a person in a great panic. But if he realizes that waves crash and that it doesn't really matter if the whole human race blows up, then there's a chance he won't push the button. It is the only chance we have to avoid doing this thing that attracts us so powerfully, like a kind of vertigo. Or the way a person who looks over a precipice is attracted to the idea of throwing himself over. Or the way a skydiver sometimes forgets to pull the parachute ring, because he becomes hypnotized by the target—it's called target fascination. He just goes straight at it.

So, we can become absolutely fascinated with disaster and doom. That is why all the news in the newspapers is invariably bad news. There's no good news in newspapers. People wouldn't buy a newspaper consisting of good news.

Our fascination with doom might be neutralized if we would realize that every new doom is just another fluctuation in the huge, marvelous, endless chain of our own selves and our own energy.

Our problem is that, because of our myopia—because of the way we focus our consciousness upon that certain little area of experience we call voluntary action—we think that we are no more than that and that everything else just happens to us. But that is obviously absurd.

Pick up a gyroscopic top. You will notice, the minute you get it in your hand, that it has a kind of vitality to it. It seems to resist you. It starts pushing you in a certain way, just as if it were a living animal you were holding in your hand. Pick up a hamster or a guinea pig, and it always tries to escape. The gyroscope always seems to be trying to escape your hold, too.

In that same way, what you are experiencing all the time in life are all sorts of things getting out of control and doing things you don't expect. It is as if something's trying to escape your hold. But if you don't grab it too hard, you will discover that this thing that you are feeling, that feels like a gyroscope, is your own life.

You cannot understand the experience that you call voluntary action or decision or being in control or being yourself unless there is something else in opposition to it. You couldn't realize things like self and control and will unless there were something else that is out of control—something that instead of will, won't. It is these two opposites together that produce the sensation that we call having a personal identity.

There is a funny thing about human consciousness, though, that Gestalt psychology has worked out very carefully. It is that our attention is captured by the figure rather than the background and by the relatively enclosed area rather than the diffuse area and by something that's moving rather than something that is still. To all the phenomena that attract our attention in this way, we attribute a higher degree of reality than we do to the things we don't notice.

Consciousness is a radar device that is scanning the environment to look out for trouble, just in the same way as a ship's radar is looking for rocks or other ships. And the radar therefore does not notice the vast areas of space where there are no rocks or ships. In the same way, our eyes—or rather the selective consciousness behind our eyes—pay attention only to what we think is important.

As I speak, I am aware of all of you in this room, of every single detail of your clothing, of your faces, and so on. But I am not noticing those details at all, and tomorrow I will not be able to remember exactly how each one of you looks today. What I notice is restricted to things that I think are important.

If I notice a particularly beautiful person in the audience, then that would be memorable, and I might also notice what that person is wearing. But by and large, we scan everything, but pay attention only to what our set of values tells us we ought to pay attention to. Obviously, you as a complete individual are much more than this scanning system, and you as a complete individual are in relationships with the external world that on the whole are incredibly harmonious.

Going back to the idea that the living body is like the flame of a candle, we can say that the energies of life—in the forms of temperature, light, air, food, and so on—are streaming through us all at this moment in the most magnificently harmonious way. And all of us are far more beautiful than any candle flame. Only, we are so used to our harmony and beauty that we say, "So what? Show me something interesting. Show me something new." It is a characteristic of consciousness that it ignores stimuli that are constant. When anything is constant, consciousness says, "Okay, that's safe. It's in the bag. I needn't pay attention to that anymore." And therefore we systematically eliminate from our awareness all the gorgeous things that are going on all the time, and instead we focus only on the troublesome things that might upset us.

The problem is, we make too much of it. And because we do, we identify our very self—our *I*, our ego—with the radar, the troubleshooter. And the troubleshooter is only a tiny fragment of our total being.

Now, if you become aware that you are not simply that scanning mechanism, that you are your complete organism, then you will become aware that your organism is not what you thought it was when you looked at it from the standpoint of conscious attention or from the standpoint of the ego. From the standpoint of the ego, your organism is a kind of vehicle, an automobile within which you move around. From a physical point of view, your organism is like a candle flame or a whirlpool. It is part of the continuous, patterning activity of the whole cosmos.

The key idea here is pattern.

I want to borrow a metaphor from the architect Buckminster Fuller. Imagine that we have a rope of many sections. The first section is made of manila hemp, and the next is made of cotton, and the next is made of silk, and the next is nylon, and so on. We tie an ordinary overhand knot in this rope. By putting our finger in the knot, we can move that knot all the way down the rope. As the knot travels, it's first made out of manila hemp, then of cotton, then of silk, and then nylon, and so on. But the knot remains a knot. That's the integrity of pattern, of all patterns, including the continuing pattern that is you.

You might be a vegetarian for several years, and then you might become a meat eater. In any case, your constitution changes all the time, but still your friends recognize you, because you are still putting on the same show, you are still the same pattern. And that is what makes you a recognizable individual.

The very structure of the language we speak deceives us into misunderstanding this, however. When we see a pattern we ask, "What is it made of?" We see a table and we ask whether it is made of wood or aluminum. But when we ask what wood is made of, and how it differs from aluminum, the only answer a scientist can give is that they are two different patterns. That is to say, the molecular structures of the two are different. And a molecular structure is not a description of what something is made of, it is a description of the dance it is performing, of the symphony that it is.

All the phenomena of life are musical. Gold differs from lead in exactly the same way that a waltz differs from a mazurka. They are different dances. And there isn't any *thing* that's dancing. The belief that some thing is dancing is a deception we fall into because of our language. It has nouns and verbs in it. And verbs are supposed to describe the activities of nouns. But this is simply a convention of speech. A language could be made entirely out of verbs. You don't really need nouns. Or you could have a language made entirely of nouns, without verbs. And it would adequately describe what's going on in the world.

If you were to speak a language composed of one part of speech, you would be able to say just as much as you can with two, and it would be a lot clearer. At first it would sound awkward, but you would soon get used to it. And when you did, it would become a matter of common sense that the patterning of the world is not the result of some thing that's patterning and that there's no substance underlying everything. There are just patterns.

Existence, for a person who really wakes up, does not consist of being a hopeless little creature confronted by a big external world that growls at it and eats it up. Every tiny little thing that comes into being, every minute fruit fly or gnat or bacterium, is an event on which this whole cosmos depends.

And that dependency goes both ways. Every little organism depends on its total environment for its existence, and the total environment depends on the existence of each and every one of those little organisms. Therefore, you could say that this universe consists of an arrangement of patterns in which every pattern is essential to the existence of the whole.

Now, we screen that idea out of our consciousness, just as we screen out the fact that space is an important reality. We pay attention to the figure and ignore the background. And so we believe that organisms are very frail and the environment is very strong. The environment lasts a long time, after all, but organisms exist for only a short time.

But what does the environment consist of? Just a lot of little things. The environment exists in just the same way that a face exists in a newspaper photograph. When you get far enough away from the tiny dots that comprise the photo, you can see the face. In the same way, when you get far enough away from all the organisms and the little bits of matter—when you change the scale of magnification—you can see the environment.

The whole environment is arranged in a system of polarities, in which the enormous depends on the tiny and the tiny depends on the enormous. There is a relationship between those extremes that can be called a transaction, similar to a financial transaction. It is impossible to have buying without selling or selling without buying. They always go together. But, of course, the person who is interested in buying tends to think more about buying than he does about selling. But if he doesn't think about the mechanisms that the other fellow is using to sell, he's going to get a bad deal. And if I want to sell something, and I think too much about selling, I won't enter sufficiently into the psychology of the buyer and I won't get the best deal for myself. I won't be a good business shark.

In this way, we always tend to overemphasize a certain aspect of our experience. In the West, there is a unique emphasis on individuality. We have made an immense psychic investment in our own individuality. We ask ourselves what are we going to amount to? What are we going to contribute to human life? What is our particular destiny?

Individuality is a fine idea, but the thing we don't understand about it is that it won't work unless it is balanced by its opposite. Just as you can't have a back without a front, you cannot have individuality without commonality. By this I mean having another level of being at which there is no individuality at all, at which I am you and you are me.

Everyone feels that he is the center of the universe, and that everything else is happening in a circle around him. It is literally true that we can turn around and see equally far in all directions, especially if we are on a ship in the middle of the ocean. In fact, we live in a curved space–time continuum, which is a universe at which every point may be regarded as the center of the universe.

Consider a sphere. Which point on its surface is the center of its surface? You can see at once that any point can be the center. So, legitimately, each point in the universe is the center. That's St. Bonaventure's description of God: "That circle whose center is everywhere and whose circumference is nowhere." Everybody is in this situation.

At that depth of existence, we are all like the nerve ends on our own skin. At every point on our skin, there are little nerve endings gathering information from the outside world. Together, these nerve endings constitute our total sensitivity. In the same way, people, with their little eyes and ears, are all really one common center called I, which is looking at itself from ever so many different points of view.

We are so close to the center, though, and we are so absorbed in the different ways each one of us is occupying the center, that we neglect the underlying community that links us together. Individuality emerges from that community.

It's all a matter of scale.

When you get to a certain level of scale, individuality emerges from the communal background. If something with an entirely different form of biology were to come to this planet, it wouldn't know the difference between Africans, Greeks, Armenians, or Anglo-Saxons. We would all look exactly the same to it.

You can take flatworms and teach them certain tricks. If you put them in a blender, pulverize them, and feed them to untrained flatworms, the new flatworms acquire the old flatworms' tricks. Maybe one day we will take DNA from geniuses and feed it to average people and turn them into geniuses. Think of that. But the point of talking about pulverized flatworms is to show that what is transmitted is the repetition of pattern, the repetition of certain rhythms.

The great Dutch artist Escher has a book of the most fantastic patterns. One drawing may show, for example, an arrangement of devils, but when you look at the background, you see it's an arrangement of angels. In his work, everything goes with its counterpoint, so that when you look at one of his pictures you don't know what is the foreground and what is the background. You just flip, flip, flip, flip between the two, and you can see the picture either way.

Everything is like that. But we are too fascinated

by whatever we, at any given moment, have selected to be the foreground to be aware of that. The foreground comes before; it is important. The background—oh, it's just background. And so, we frequently can't see the forest for the trees or the trees for the forest.

Whenever you are looking at the general panorama of sensory experience, try switching foreground and background. Try shifting your attention from all the things you think are important to all the things you think are unimportant. Look at the constants, the background. Look at the spaces *between* people, for instance.

All painters have to learn this, because they actually have to paint the background. Weavers know this, too, because when they are making patterns in weaving, they've got to weave the background as well. The people who made the great Oriental carpets were very aware that the background constitutes an essential part of the total experience of the carpet.

And so, as you become aware of backgrounds, you will notice the same thing that one notices in music: It is only as a result of hearing the interval between tones that one hears the melody. If you don't hear the interval, you will miss the rhythm and all the notes will sound like the same noise with variations in tone. To hear the melody, you've got to hear the intervals between the notes. Similarly, you've got to watch the intervals between people—the things that aren't said and the things that are implicit. And then you will begin to be connected.

It is very important to have a connection with life and to be in the know. And the fundamental way to discover that connection is to look at and see the things you usually forget or ignore. But that is the hardest thing in the world to do. And what is the most obvious thing we forget? It's the answer to the question: Who do I think I am?

How do we normally answer that question? We say our name. I'm Alan Watts. But that's not the true answer. That's only what people have told us we are. They put our names on us, and they teach us to identify with them. But we are not our names.

We know this very well. If we go back in memory to our infancy, to before people started telling us all this stuff, we will see very well who we are: the jolly old Ancient of Days. Because everybody is.

If one person realizes it and another doesn't, though, the other is a little bit offended. That's a problem. We solved it in Christianity by the very clever idea of allowing only one individual to be recognized as the Ancient of Days, as God incarnate. And since he has been safely crucified and whisked up to heaven, he can't offend us anymore. And everyone who feels an intimation of who they really are—God incarnate—and says it out loud, within Christianity, gets criticized: "Who the hell do you think you are, anyway? Jesus Christ?"

Actually, even when Jesus Christ himself said he was Jesus Christ, everybody put him down. But Christians did allow him to say who he was; they did allow that one person, that one human individual, to be the incarnation of God—but only him. In our theory of the universe, the individual is simply involved in something that is happening to him. And we feel that this thing that happens to us is reality, and that reality is something other than us. We don't recognize it as an integral part of our own being, without which we cannot know what we mean by the word *I*. But if we face the truth, every single one of us will know that there is a recess of the soul, of the psyche, where everybody understands perfectly that he is not just an irresponsible little mouse that's been shot out into the world, but that he is really running the world.

The problem is we can't admit it, in the same way we can't admit that we are responsible for the way our own hearts beat. We say, "Oh, that's not my doing. I have no control over my heart." But do you have any control over anything? Do you have control over being conscious, for instance? Do we know how we perform an act of will? We say, "I will my hand to move from my face to my leg." We can do that, but we don't know how it is done.

Therefore, we do not understand at all what we mean by voluntary control. We might even say that the only kind of control we really understand is the kind in which we do not use our will at all. We just open and close our hand. We know how to do it, but we can't explain to someone how to do it. And we don't realize that, just as we know how to open and close our hand, we know equally well how to turn the sun into light and make the sky blue and blow the wind and wave the ocean. Just as we know how to digest food and how to be digested and transformed by bacteria. As we transform our steaks, so will we, in turn, be transformed. The patterns will continue, and the pattern is always you.

We have the marvelous capacity to transform ourselves without knowing that we are doing it and therefore to keep on surprising ourselves and therefore to keep on doing what we do. Because if we didn't surprise ourselves, we wouldn't keep on doing it. It is the very fact that we seem to be the victims of the things that happen that we don't understand and that we seem to come to an end every time we die, that allows us to be alive. Every time life happens to us, it is as if it had never happened to us before. Every time we are born, it seems that we are being born for the first time. But, of course, if it didn't, we wouldn't keep on letting it happen to us.

FROM TIME
TO ETERNITY

CHAPTER FOUR

hen St. Augustine of Hippo was asked, "What is time?" he replied, "I know what it is, but when you ask me, I don't." Amusingly enough, he is the man most responsible for the commonsensical idea of time that prevails in the West.

The Greeks and East Indians thought of time as a circular process. Anyone looking at a watch will obviously see that time goes around. But the Hebrews and the Christians thought of time as something that goes in a straight line. And that is a powerful idea, which influences everybody living in the West today.

CHAPTER FOUR

We all have our various mythologies. When I use the word *mythology*, or *myth*, I don't mean something that is false. I mean an idea or an image by which people make sense of the world.

The Western myth, under which our common sense has been nurtured over many centuries, is that the world began in the year 4000 B.C. This myth is presented in the King James Bible, which descended from heaven with an angel in the year 1611. According to this myth, the Lord God naturally had existed forever and ever and ever, through endless time. The world was created, and then it fell apart. And so, in the middle of time, the second person of the Trinity incarnated himself in the form of Jesus Christ in order to save mankind and establish the true Church. Sometime in the future, time will come to an end. There will be a day that will be the Last Day, in which the second person of the Trinity— God the Son—will appear again in glory with his legions of angels. And the Last Judgment will be held. And those who are saved will live forever and ever in contemplation of the vision of the Blessed Trinity. And those who did not behave themselves will squirm forever in hell.

Time, according to this presentation, is unidirectional. Each event happens once, and it can never be repeated. According to St. Augustine, when God the Son came into this world, he sacrificed himself for the remission of all sins. That was an event that could happen once and only once.

I don't know why he thought that, but he sure did think it. And so we have the idea that time is a unique story that had a definite beginning and is going to have a definite end, and that's that. Most Westerners do not believe in this story anymore, although many of them think that they ought to believe in it. But even though they don't believe in it, they still retain from it a way of thinking, a linear view of time, that says that we are going down a one-way road. We will never again go back over the course that we have followed. And we hope, as we go on, that in time, things will get progressively better and better.

This version of time differs in a very strange and fascinating way from the view of time held by most other people in the world. Take the Hindu view of time. The Hindus are not so small-minded and provincial as to believe that the world was created as recently as 4000 B.C. They calculate the ages of the universe in units of four million, three hundred and twenty thousand years. That is their basic counting unit, and it is called a *kalpa*. And so, their understanding of the world is quite different from ours.

We in the West think of the world as an artifact, made by a grand technician, the Creator. But the Hindus do not think that the world was created at all. They look upon it as a drama—not as having been created, but as being acted. They see God as the supreme actor, or as what is called the cosmic self, playing all the different parts simultaneously. In other words, you and the birds and bees and flowers and rocks and stars are all an act put on by God, who is pretending to be all these things, through the many eternities, in order to amuse himself. He is pretending that he is all of us. And this is not, after all, such an unreasonable idea. If I were to ask you to consider what you would do if you were God, you might find that being omniscient and all-powerful and eternal would eventually become extremely boring. Eventually you would want a surprise.

What are we trying to do with our technology? We are trying to control the world. We are trying to become all-powerful and omniscient. Imagine the ultimate fulfillment of that desire. When we are in control of every-thing and we have great panels of push buttons whereby the slightest touch fulfills every wish, what will we want then? We will eventually want to arrange to have a spe-cial, red button marked "surprise" built into the panel. Touch that button and what happens? We will suddenly disappear from our normal consciousness and find our-selves in a situation very much like the one we are now in, where we feel ourselves to be a little bit out of con-trol, subject to surprises, and subject to the whims of an unpredictable universe.

The Hindus figure that God presses the surprise button every so often. That is to say, for a period of four million, three hundred and twenty thousand years, God knows who He is. And then He gets bored with that and forgets who He is for an equal period of four million, three hundred and twenty thousand years. He goes to sleep and has a dream, and this dream is called the *Manvantara*. The period in which He wakes up and is not dreaming is called the *Pralaya*, a state of total bliss. But when He has a dream, He manifests the world.

This manifestation of the world is divided into four ages. They are named after the four throws in the Indian game of dice. The first throw is *krita*, which is the throw of four, the perfect throw. The *Krita-yuga*, or first age, lasts for a very long time.

In this period of the manifestation of the world, everything is absolutely delightful. It would be the same, for example, if you had the privilege of dreaming any dream you wanted to dream when you went to sleep at night. For at least a month you would live out all your wishes in your dreams. You would have banquets and music and everything that you ever thought you wanted.

But then, after a few weeks of this, you would say, "Well, this is getting a little dull. Let's have an adventure. Let's get into trouble." It is all right to get into trouble because you know you are going to wake up at the end of it. So you could fight dragons and rescue princesses, and all that sort of thing.

After awhile, when that got boring, you could get more and more far out. You could arrange to forget that you were dreaming. You would believe you really were involved in danger, and what a surprise it would be when you woke up. And then, one of those nights, when you were dreaming any dream you wanted to dream, you would even find yourself sitting where you are right now, with all your special problems and hang-ups and reading and involvement, reading these words. How do you know that that is not what is happening?

So then, after the Krita-yuga in which everything is perfect, there comes a somewhat shorter epoch called the *Treta-yuga*, named after the throw of three in the Hindu game of dice. And in the Treta-yuga, things are a little bit less secure.

When that epoch comes to an end, there comes the third: a shorter period called the *Dvapara-yuga*—named after *dva*, the throw of two. In this period, the forces of good and evil are equally balanced.

When that era comes to an end, there follows a still shorter period called the *Kali-yuga*. *Kali* means the throw of one, or the worst throw. And in this period, the forces of negation and destruction are finally triumphant.

The Kali-yuga is supposed to have started shortly before 3000 B.C. We have another five thousand years of it to go. In this period, everything falls apart, and things get worse and worse and worse, until finally, at the end, the Lord himself appears in the disguise of Kali, the destroyer. Kali is black-bodied, has four arms, and wears a necklace of skulls. In one hand, he holds a bloody sword. A second hand holds a severed head by the hair. A third hand is open, fingers extended forward in the boon-giving gesture. The fourth hand is also open, fingers pointing up, palm exposed in the gesture that means don't be afraid, everything is just a big act. Thereupon the entire cosmos is destroyed in fire, and in every soul the Lord wakes up again and discovers who He is, and abides for a Pralaya of four million, three hundred and twenty thousand years in a state of total bliss.

This sequence of eras repeats forever. It is the in-breathing and out-breathing of Brahma, the supreme self. And they add up into years of Brahma, each one of which is three hundred and sixty kalpas. And these in turn add up again into centuries, and it goes on and on and on. But it never gets boring because every time the new Manvantara starts, the Lord God forgets everything that happened before and becomes completely absorbed in the act, just as you did when you were born and you opened your eyes on the world for what you thought was the first time. All the world was strange and wonderful. You saw it with the clear eyes of a child.

Of course, as you get older, you get more used to things. You have seen the sun again and again, and you think it is just the same old sun. You have seen the trees until you regard them as the same old trees. And finally, you begin to get bored and you start to fall apart and disintegrate until you die because you have had enough of it. But then after you die, another baby is born who is of course you, because every baby calls itself I and sees the whole thing from a new point of view again, and is perfectly thrilled. And so in this way, arranged wonderfully, so that there is never any absolutely intolerable boredom, the time goes on and on and on and around and around and around.

This Hindu myth is one of the great myths of time in the world. And we, in our day and age, need to consider this myth very seriously. As a highly technological civilization with enormous power over nature, we really need to consider time. Therefore, let me ask again the question that was asked of St. Augustine: "What is time?" I am not going to give you his answer. I know what time is, and when you ask me I will tell you. Time is a measure of energy, a measure of motion.

We have agreed internationally on the speed of the clock. So I want you to think about clocks and watches for a moment. We are, of course, slaves to them. And you will notice that your watch has a circular face, and that it is calibrated. Each minute or second is marked by a hairline, made as narrow as possible, while yet remaining visible. When we think of what we mean by the word "now," we think of the shortest possible instant that is here and then gone immediately, because that thought corresponds with the image of the hairline calibrations on a watch.

As a result, we are a people who feel that we don't have any present, because we believe that the present is always instantly vanishing. This is the problem of Goethe's Faust. He attains his great moment and says to it, "Oh still delay, thou art so fair." But the moment never stays. It is always disappearing into the past.

Therefore we have the sensation that our lives are constantly flowing away from us. And so we have a sense of urgency: Time is not to waste; time is money. And so, because of the tyranny of clocks, we feel that we have a past, and that we know who we were in the past—nobody can ever tell you who they *are*; they can only tell you who they *were*—and we believe we also have a future. And that belief is terribly important, because we have a naive hope that the future is somehow going to supply us with everything we're looking for.

You see, if you live in a present that is so short that it is not really there at all, you will always feel vaguely frustrated. When you ask a person, "What did you do yesterday?" he will give you a historical account of a sequence of events. He will say, "I woke up at about seven o'clock in the morning. I got up and made myself some coffee, and then I brushed my teeth and took a shower, got dressed, had some breakfast and went down to the office." He gives you a historical outline of a course of events. And people really think that is what they did.

But actually that is only a very skeletal account of what they did. People live a much richer life than that, but they don't notice it. They only pay attention to a very small part of the information received through their five senses. They forget that when they got up in the morning and made some coffee, their eyes slid across the birds outside their window. They forget about the light on the leaves of the tree and that their nose played games with the scent of the coffee. They forget because they weren't aware of it. Because they were in a hurry. They were engaged in consuming that coffee as fast as possible so that they could get to their office to do something they thought was terribly important.

And maybe it was, in a certain way; it made money. But, because they were so absorbed with the future, they had no use for the money they made. They couldn't enjoy it. Maybe they invested it so that they could have a future in which something finally might happen to them, the something that they were looking for all along. But of course, it never will happen to them, because tomorrow never comes. The truth of the matter is that there is no such thing as time. Time is a hallucination. There is only today. There never will be anything except today. And if you do not know how to live today, you are demented.

This is the great problem of Western civilization, of all civilizations. Civilization is a very complex system in which we use symbols—words, numbers, figures, and concepts—to represent the real world of nature. We use money to represent wealth. We use the clock to represent time. We use yards and inches to represent space. These are very useful measures. But you can always have too much of a good thing. You can easily confuse the measurement with what you are measuring, such as confusing money with wealth. It is like confusing the menu with the dinner. You can become so enchanted with the symbols that you entirely confuse them with the reality. This is the disease from which almost all civilized people are suffering. We are, therefore, in the position of eating the menu instead of the dinner, of living in a world of words and symbols. This causes us to relate badly to our material surroundings.

The United States of America, as the most progressive country of the West, is the great example of this. We are a people who believe ourselves to be the great materialists, and we are slightly ashamed of it. But this is an absolutely undeserved reputation. A materialist is a person who loves material and therefore reveres it, respects it, and enjoys it. We don't do that. We are a people who hate material. We're devoting ourselves to the abolition of its limitations. We want to abolish the limits of time and space. We want to get rid of space. We call it the conquest of space. We want to be able to get from San Francisco to New York in nothing flat. And we are arranging to do just that. We do not realize what the result of doing that will be: San Francisco and New York will become the same place, and then it will not be worth going from one to the other.

When you want to go on vacation, you want to go someplace that's different. You might think of Hawaii, where you imagine sandy beaches, the lovely blue ocean, and coral reefs. But tourists are increasingly asking of such a place, "Has it been spoiled yet?" By this they mean, "Is it exactly like Dallas yet?" And the answer is, "Yes." The faster you can get from Dallas to Honolulu, the faster Honolulu is becoming the same place as Dallas and the less reason there is to make the trip. Tokyo has become the same place as Los Angeles. As you go faster and faster from place to place on the earth, they are all becoming the same place. That is the result of abolishing the limitations of time and space.

We are in a hurry about too many things. Going back to my account of someone's day: The person got up in the morning and made some coffee, and I suppose it was instant coffee, because that person was in too much of a hurry to be concerned with the preparation of a beautiful cup of coffee. Instant coffee is a punishment for people who are in too much of a hurry.

This is true of everything that's instant. There is something phony and fake about it. Where were you rushing into the future? What did you think the future was going to bring you? Actually, you don't know. I've always thought it an excellent idea to assign to freshmen in college the task of writing an essay on what they would like heaven to be. In other words, to make them think about what they really want in that abstraction the future. Because the truth of the matter is this—as I have already intimated—there is no such thing as the future. Time is an abstraction. So is money, for that matter. So are inches.

Think about the Great Depression. One day everything was going along fine—everybody was pretty wealthy and had plenty to eat—and the next day, suddenly, everybody was in poverty. What happened? Had the farms disappeared? Had the cows vanished into thin air? Had the fish of the sea ceased to exist? Had human beings lost their energy, their skills, and their brains? No. This is what happened: On the morning after the beginning of the Depression, a carpenter came to work, and the foreman said to him, "Sorry, chum, you can't work today. There ain't no inches."

The carpenter said, "What do you mean, there ain't no inches?"

"Yeah," the foreman said. "We got lumber, we got metal, but we ain't got no inches."

"You're crazy," the carpenter said.

And the foreman replied, "The trouble with you is you don't understand business."

What happened in the Great Depression was that human beings confused money with wealth. And they didn't realize that money is a measure of wealth, in exactly the same way that inches are a measure of length. They think it is something that is valuable in and of itself. And as a result of that they get into unbelievable trouble.

In the same way, time is nothing but an abstract measure of motion. And we keep counting time. We have the sensation that time is running out, and we bug ourselves with this. Suppose you are working. Are you watching the clock? If you are, what are you waiting for? Time off. Five o'clock. You can go home and have fun. What are you going to do when you get home? Have fun? Or are you going to watch TV—which is an electronic reproduction of life that doesn't even smell of anything—and eat a TV dinner—which is a kind of warmed-over airline nastiness—until you just get tired and have to go to sleep?

This is our problem, you see. We are not alive. We are not awake. We are not living in the present. Take education. What a hoax. As a child, you are sent to nursery school. In nursery school, they say you are getting ready to go on to kindergarten. And then first grade is coming up and second grade and third grade. They say you are gradually climbing the ladder, making progress. And then, when you get to the end of grade school, they say, "You've been getting ready for high school." And then in high school, they tell you you're getting ready for college. And in college you're getting ready to go out into the business world with your suit and your diploma. And you go to your first sales meeting, and they say, "Now get out there and sell this stuff." They say you'll be going on up the ladder in business if you sell it, and maybe you'll get a promotion. And you sell it, and they up your quota. And then, finally at about the age of forty-five, you wake up one morning as vice president of the firm, and you say to yourself, "I've arrived. But I've been cheated. Something is missing. I no longer have a future." "Wrong," says the insurance salesman. "I have a future for you. This policy will enable you to retire in comfort at sixty-five, and now you can look forward to that." And you're delighted. You buy the policy, and at sixty-five, you retire, thinking that this is the attainment of the goal of life. Except that now you have prostate trouble, false teeth, and wrinkled skin. And you're a materialist. You're a phantom. You are an abstraction. You are nowhere, because you were never told, and you never realized, that eternity is now. There is no time.

What will you do then? Can you recover the pop of a champagne cork that popped last night? Can you hand me a copy of tomorrow's *Dallas Morning Herald*? It just isn't here. There is no time. Time is a fantasy. It is a useful fantasy, just as the lines of latitude and longitude are. But they aren't real lines. You are never going to tie up a package with the equator. It and time are the same; they're abstractions. Time is a convenience. It allows us to arrange to meet each other at the corner of Main and First at four o'clock. Great. But let us not be fooled by convenience. It is not real.

People who do not live in the present have absolutely no use for making plans. People who believe in time and who believe that they are living for their future make plenty of plans. But when the plans mature, the people are not there to enjoy them. They are planning something else. And they are like donkeys running after carrots that are hanging in front of their faces from sticks attached to their own collars. They are never here. They never get there. They are never alive. They are perpetually frustrated. And therefore they are always thinking. The future is the thing with them. Someday it is going to happen, they think. And because it never does, they are frantic. They want more time, more time, please, more time. They are terrified of death, because death stops the future. And so they never get there, wherever there is. There is always somewhere else, around the corner.

Please, wake up.

I am not saying that you should be improvident, that you shouldn't have an insurance policy, that you shouldn't be concerned about how you are going to send your children to college. Except that there is no point in sending your children to college and providing for their future if you don't know how to live in the present, because all you will do is teach your children how not to live in the present. You will end up dragging yourself through life for the alleged benefit of your own children, who will in turn drag out their lives in a boring way for the alleged benefit of their children.

Everybody is looking after everybody else so beautifully that nobody has any fun at all. We say of a person who is insane that he is not all here. Not being all here is our collective disease.

In the beginning of the regime of communism in Russia, they had five-year plans, and everything was going to be great at the end of the five years, except that when they got to the end, they had to make another five-year plan. They were making human beings into a floor on which the next generation would dance. But, of course, the next generation wouldn't be able to dance; it would have to become the floor for the generation after that. And so on. Each generation holds up the floor above it, forever and ever, and nobody ever dances.

But you see, the philosophy of the communists and our philosophy is exactly the same. In fact, our system is their system. And increasingly, we and they are becoming more and more alike, because of our misperception of the reality of time. We are obsessed with time. It is always coming. Mao Tse-tung can say to all the Chinese, "Live a great boring life and wear the same clothes and carry around a little red book and one day, perhaps, everything will be great."

And we are in exactly the same situation. We are the richest people in the world, and most of our businessmen go around in dark suits looking like undertakers. We eat Wonder Bread, which is styrofoam injected with some chemicals that are supposed to be nutritious. We do not even know how to eat. In other words, we live in the abstract, not in the concrete. We work for money, not for wealth. We look forward to the future and do not know how to enjoy today. And we are destroying our environment. We are Los Angelizing the world, instead of civilizing it. We are turning the air into gas fumes and the water into poison. We are tearing the vegetation off the face of the hills. And for what? To print newspapers.

In our colleges, we value the record of what has happened more than we value what is happening. The records in the registrar's office are kept in safes under lock and key, but not the books in the library. What you do is, of course, much more important than what you did. We don't understand this. We go out on a picnic, and somebody says, "We are having a lovely time. What a pity somebody didn't bring a camera." People go on tours with wretched little boxes around their necks, and instead of being in the scene, whatever it is, they go click, click, click with those little boxes so that when they get home they can show photographs to their friends and say, "See what happened. Of course I wasn't really there, I was just photographing it."

When the record becomes more important than the event, we are really up the creek with no paddle. So the most serious need of civilization is to come to now. Think of all the trouble we would save. Think of how peaceful things would become. We would not be inter- fering with everybody. We would not be doing every- body else good, like the general who destroyed a village in Vietnam for its own safety. That is the explanation he gave. "Kindly let me help you or you will drown," said the monkey, putting the fish safely up a tree.

Now is the meaning of eternal life. Jesus said, "Before Abraham was, I am." He didn't say "I was." He said, "I am." And to come to this, to know that you are and there is no time except the present, is to suddenly attain a sense of reality.

The aim of education ought to be to teach people to live in the present, to be all here. Instead, our educa- tional system is pretty abstract. It neglects the absolute fundamentals of life and instead teaches us to be bureau- crats, bank clerks, accountants, and insurance salesmen. It entirely neglects our relationships to the material world of which there are five: farming, cooking, cloth- ing, housing, and lovemaking. These are grossly over- looked. And so it becomes possible for the Congress of the United States to pass a law making it a grave penalty for anyone to burn the flag. Yet those same congressmen, by acts of commission or omission, are responsible for burning up what the flag stands for and for the erosion of the natural resources of this land. Although they say they love their country, they don't. Their country is a reality. They love their flag, which is an abstraction. So I think it is time to get back to reality, to get back from time to eternity, to get back to the eternal now, which is what we have, always have had, and indeed always will have.

THE SMELL OF BURNT ALMONDS

CHAPTER FIVE

A lmost all the great religions of the world are, in some way, associated with a drink—Judaism and Christianity with wine, Islam with coffee, Hinduism with the milk of sacred cows, Buddhism with tea. And in one way or another, these sacred drinks are used for sacramental purposes. The sacrament, as it is defined in the Anglican Church, is the outward and visible sign of an inward and spiritual grace. It is a very common feature of religion throughout the world, although one which is highly disapproved of by many people living today in the Western world under the influence of Protestantism and Humanism.

The sacrament, in other words, is a method of giving spiritual power or insight through corporeal means. For example, in the sacrament of baptism, orthodox Christians believe that through the pouring on of water—a physical substance—a person may be in some way united with the grace of God. As another example, some believe that the right words said by the right person over bread and wine transform the bread into the body of Christ and the wine into the blood of Christ. Furthermore, whoever partakes of them—on the principle that you are what you eat—is transformed into Christ.

Behind the more obvious drinks of sacramental liquids associated with the various religions, there are some religions that employ more potent substances. One associates Islam and the whole Arabic culture with the use of hashish. No one who knows anything about the effects of this substance can doubt that the people who painted Persian miniatures and who designed the great arabesques of Islamic civilization had the sort of vision that comes with using hashish.

Likewise, the earliest Vedic texts of India mention something called *soma*. Nobody really knows what soma was, but one may guess, in view of modern practices in India, that it was either a brew derived from cannabis, which today is used by certain types of yogi, or a concoction of psychoactive mushrooms. Shiva worshippers use cannabis widely in the form of *bung*, which is a drink, or *gangia*, which is smoked.

In China, there was for a long time a quest for the elixir of life in the Taoist school of philosophy. This was associated with alchemy, but when you read alchemical texts, you must realize that they are always veiled. The Taoist sages were apparently looking for an elixir of immortality that would convert a human being into an immortal. It was supposed that if you drank the right elixir, when you became an old man, your shriveled skin would peel off and reveal a youth underneath, as a snake changes its skin. We find statues in certain parts of China of venerable old sages with their skin falling off to reveal a young face below, and many sages—indeed even emperors—died from drinking concoctions that purported to be the elixir of life.

One of the ingredients of the elixir was always tea, but of course tea, as drunk in Buddhist circles, is not the tea that you ordinarily drink. The real ceremonial tea of the Far East is not steeped tea leaves, but green tea ground to a very fine powder. Hot water is poured over it, and then it is stirred with a whisk into a thick mixture. Drinking a few cups of this puts you in a state of extraordinary wakefulness and, therefore, has long been used by Buddhist monks for purposes of meditation. Tea of this sort has a mild psychedelic or consciousness-expanding effect. The Tibetans likewise brew an incredibly thick tea that they mix with yak butter. To us it is an appalling concoction, but to them very soothing and comforting and also wakeful.

Throughout the cultures of Native Americans, religion is centered around divine plants. Native Americans use the peyote cactus, yagé, mushrooms such as *Psylicibin mexicana*, the jimson weed or datura, and a considerable number of other plants that have been catalogued by Professor Schultz of Harvard. Even some seaweeds are considered divine plants. The mushroom *Psylicibin mexicana* is known among certain Native Americans as "the flesh of God."

To an enormous degree, throughout the world, going back as far as we can find any record, there has been the use of some sort of plant—either chewed or distilled or boiled—that transformed consciousness and was alleged to give mankind the vision of divine things. Objection to the use of sacramental plants is very strong in the modern West, and there have always been people who deplored this kind of practice. It must be said in the modern West that the use of any material aid to spiritual insight or development is looked upon with disfavor, because it is seen as a crutch. And culture feels happier if it doesn't use a crutch—in other words, if you do it yourself. Somehow or other, the use of a crutch—or as people call it with that question-begging word *drug*—seems to be something that is a sign of weakness. If you are a gutsy fellow and you are going to get this vision in a manner that is natural and legitimate—so that it will really stay with you—you ought to work at it by your own efforts.

You will find this exemplified in Christian Science, a religion that prohibits the use of any medicine for physical health. However, every Christian Scientist is dependent on daily food, both vegetables and meats, and eats them without any feeling of guilt. He ought to realize that if he had sufficient faith, he would be able to live without food or air.

I suppose it sounds farfetched to say that air is a crutch on which we depend or that the earth is a lamentable ball on which we have to stand in order to hold ourselves up. But if you explore deeply the doctrines and history of almost any religion, you will find that there is simply no do-it-yourself way. Whatever path you follow, invariably you reach a point at which the efforts of your own will or your own ego have to be abandoned.

In Japanese Buddhism, there are two schools: *Jiriki* and *Tariki*. Jiriki means one's own power. Tariki means another's power. Most forms of Buddhism are classified as Jiriki on the principle of the Buddha's final words to his disciples, "Be ye a refuge unto yourselves.

Take to yourselves no other refuge, and work out your own deliverance with diligence." And so in Zen and in *Tendai*, in the *Theravadan*, or southern forms of Buddhism, you will find that meditation practice or spiritual growth is a matter of using relentless effort to control the mind. But as you concentrate and this effort develops, you reach an impasse in which your will and your ego come to a state of absolute frustration, and you find that there is nothing that you can do to reform yourself, to make yourself unselfish. You discover that, not only is there nothing that you can do, but there is also nothing that you cannot do. In other words, your exerted energy will be as phony as your attempt at re-laxation. At this point in the process of yoga or medita-tion, there must transpire a state of surrender, a total giving up. And it is precisely at this moment that the transformation of consciousness, which all these various religions are after, can come about.

In one way or another, all of the religions of the world are concerned with achieving a state of conscious-ness that is not egocentric, so that we may see through the trick that, during the egocentric state, we always play on ourselves. And the trick that we play on our-selves is that we become unable to be aware of the rela-tivity of opposites. Black and white, light and darkness, good and evil, pleasure and pain, life and death—or even oneself and the external world—in the egocentric state of consciousness seem to be separate and opposed to each other. However, the most elementary logic should tell us that opposites necessarily go together. In other words, if you feel you are a superior person in any way—morally, intellectually, or physically—you have no means of knowing that you're a superior person, except through the presence of relatively inferior people. Were they to disappear you would be left in limbo, and you

69

wouldn't know where you were at all. The higher always depends on the lower in the same way that the flower depends on the soil and the rose on the manure. So, too, the subjective self goes along with the objective, because thoughts are physical events as well as subjective ideas. Everything the self knows is in an inseparable union with the self, but we have managed to screen this out of our normal consciousness and to conduct our lives as if we could make white exist without black, light without darkness, and pleasure without pain.

When the egocentric state is surpassed, it becomes apparent that these things all go together, and the curious consequence of this is that you see the unity of all opposites, that the world is a thing of glory. It is very difficult to explain that transformation logically, but it simply is so with this different kind of consciousness. In other words, everything that you tried formerly to exclude and deny and overcome is seen to be part of a continuous construction, so that the whole world is seen as profoundly harmonious. Everything in it is exactly as it should be.

This is difficult to explain to people who don't see it, and so many people who have this kind of experience remain tongue-tied. Not only is it difficult to explain to ordinary people, but it is very shocking to ordinary people because it seems to undermine all the game rules of the social order. To say that evil things are perfectly all right because they are actually in a secret harmony with good things challenges our ideas of morality. If you are not an intelligent or sensitive person and you understand this idea superficially, you might indeed run amok. This idea could be used to justify any kind of conduct whatsoever on the grounds that everything is part of a universal harmony. This is why, through all the centuries, there has been a kind of esotericism attached to these deep matters.

A kind of secrecy surrounds both the state of consciousness itself and the various means of bringing it about, whether those means are sacramental or some form of meditation, prayer, or other type of spiritual discipline. Let me remind you that there has always been a certain secrecy surrounding this kind of knowledge. Traditionally, these things have not been taught to people or given to people who were inadequately prepared.

This is a grave problem in the modern world, because there are very few secrets in today's world. Scientific knowledge of any kind is public knowledge, at least among scientists. Of course there are types of scientific knowledge that lay people simply cannot understand because the language in which this knowledge is expressed has to be learned and is difficult to master. Many popularizations of scientific ideas are at least partial falsifications because these ideas cannot be said in English or French or German, even though they may be expressed in algebra. So in a way, all knowledge guards itself, because to understand it you have to follow, to some extent, the path that was followed by the people who discovered it.

Nevertheless, as a result of scientific technology in the modern world, an enormous number of very dangerous things are made available to fools, including the fantastic powers of destruction that technology has given us. So it is very difficult indeed to keep secrets in this day and age. Everything has been published, and practically all the mysteries have been let out of the bag. In the view of ancient Hindu philosophers, this would be regarded as a sign of the final decadence of the world and of the coming on of the Kali-yuga: the black, destructive epoch at the end of the cycle in which the whole world is destroyed.

Even those religious or spiritual disciplines that believe in an extreme exertion of the will—those Jiriki or self-power disciplines—eventually come to a point that is the same as the Tariki—those that rely on a power outside the individual will that is deeper than the personal ego. Both types of disciplines come to the same place. The difference between the two schools depends on the definition of oneself. If you start out by defining yourself as your ego, then what is other than you—or a greater power than you—will seem to be different from you. However, if you start out by defining yourself as something more than your ego, then the power that transforms you will still be your own.

For example, most people define their hearts as something other than themselves. We say, "I have a heart," rather than, "I am a heart." For most of us, the heart is an engine that somehow supports the existence of the ego. It is an engine that goes on inside us, like the engine in our car, which—if you're not a mechanic—you don't really understand. You just use it, and so you think of your heart as other than you. It is something that mysteriously happens inside you, but is beyond your control. On the other hand, if you regard your heart as the center of your physical being and very much you, then you become accustomed to thinking that when you beat your heart, you are doing it.

People who come from the Judeo-Christian philosophical traditions are inclined to feel that their heart is not themselves. The Psalmist says, "Behold, I am fearfully and wonderfully made." He looks at his own body and is astounded. And since he does not understand it, it must be the work of a God who is other than himself.

On the other hand, when a Hindu defines himself, he doesn't define himself merely in terms of those types of behavior that are voluntary. He defines himself also in terms of involuntary behavior, and so his heart seems as much himself as anything can be.

So it is really a matter of semantics as to what is self and what is other within you. It depends on where you draw the line. But it seems certain that in all spiritual traditions there comes a point at which the personal ego, the individual will, reaches its limit by one means or another. And at this point it is transformed by something that is not willed, but seems to happen spontaneously. The Christians call it grace. The Hindus call it *prajna*. The Buddhists call it *bodhi*. But in every case, it happens of itself. As the Chinese would say, "It is self-so," or itself so—or spontaneous.

So there are really no grounds for objecting to sacraments. They are something that come to us from the outside and do something to us which is beyond the control—and understanding—of the will. It has always been that way.

However, this is not an experience in which the will and the ego have no part to play. Mystical experience is that transformation of consciousness that produces the sense of union with the divine. However obtained, it is essential that initiates to this experience be grounded—that is, brought down to earth and harmonized with everyday life and human society. This requires a discipline, and every tradition looks with disfavor upon those who simply steal the divine secrets and enjoy them without some accompanying kind of discipline. Therefore, the destructive effects of methods used to achieve an altered state of consciousness are particularly problematic for people who have no capacity for the kind of discipline that must go along with their use. This is true not only of sacraments, divine plants, and yoga practices, but all things in which we might find joy. In fact, enjoyment of any kind is really impossible without some sort of an accompanying discipline.

Just think of a few things that are pleasurable and can be simply snatched and swallowed. Start with candy. Would there be such a thing as a palatable candy bar if there were not some expert in the making of sweets? And think of wine. It isn't just alcohol that one throws down. It is a skillfully prepared drink that results from a long tradition of discipline in the vintner's art. Consider racing along in a fast car. You will have an exceedingly short career in this thrilling sport if you don't know how to drive with expertise. And the car itself depends on the skill of a master mechanic.

I cannot think of anything pleasurable that does not require an accompanying discipline—even sex. A lot of people do take sex for granted, and I guess they get a kick out of it. But sex has no profound pleasure unless there is the discipline of an intimate relationship with another human being, which requires a great deal of work and intelligence. The physical aspect of sex is also a considerable art, which very few people ever seem to learn. That is why our culture has sex on the brain. We think about it perpetually. And the reason we are obsessed with sex in a voyeuristic way is because we derive so little satisfaction from it and we exhibit so little discipline and knowledge of how to use it.

So every pleasure involves a method of grounding it and integrating it with everything else. There are ways to attain what is potentially the greatest delight of all: the sense of the divine, the sense of transcending the gulf between the individual and the eternal universe. If you snatch pleasure and experience that pleasure, but you don't do anything with it or you are not properly prepared for it, you are liable to get into trouble. For that reason, psychedelic substances, the chemicals derived from the divine plants, are dangerous. There is no question about it. This is especially true of substances like

LSD, which produce their effects as a result of taking an extremely small quantity. If you want to get drunk on beer, you have to put down quite a bit of it, and there is a limit to how much beer one can swallow in an evening. But you don't have that kind of limitation with far more potent substances. The way the Native Americans take peyote cactus makes it pretty difficult to eat. It is nauseating, even though they get used to it. You must chew all that cactus, and so there is a limit to what you can swallow. But with these highly refined elixirs, there is no obvious limit. Our culture is full of downright goofy people who will try anything, even if they don't know anything about it. And the present state of affairs in the United States regarding the whole matter of psychedelic substances is in such confusion, it defies description.

These substances are called drugs, but this is a word that is not clearly defined. There is no obvious line that can be drawn between a drug and something used for food, like vitamins. A group of physicians and a group of lawyers got together not so long ago to see if they could arrive at a legal definition of addiction—that is to say, dependence on some chemical. They kept finding that whenever they thought they were close to the definition, their definition could also be applied to dependence on a foodstuff. So, this is a very difficult thing to define.

There are wide differences between various types of chemicals that produce changes in consciousness. All of them could be said to be addictive in at least a psychological sense. For example, suppose you belong to an in-group where taking LSD is *de rigueur*, and you know it is the thing to do. Soon everybody in the group is comparing notes as to how often and how much they take. You engage in this one-upmanship. This is asinine because it proves that you are following the practice simply to remain in the in-group. If you had disciplined yourself in the use of consciousness transformation, you would have soon come to see the folly of belonging to an in-group. And this is only one of many examples of how individuals and groups of people become psychologically dependent on drugs.

Other substances are addictive in a much more physical sense. Opiates, for example, cause very difficult withdrawal symptoms if one doesn't use them constantly. However, this addictive factor is not characteristic of most substances used for this purpose. In other words, most substances used for the expansion of consciousness are not narcotic. The word *narcotic* means sleep-inducing or soporific, and narcotics dull or dim the senses. Alcohol, in sufficient quantity, is a narcotic. Opium, likewise, is a narcotic. It is used for dulling the sense of pain, and its derivative, morphine, is a narcotic in the strictest sense of the word.

However, substances such as mescaline, which is the derivative of peyote or a chemical synthesis of peyote, is not a narcotic. LSD is not a narcotic. Psylicibin from the mushroom is not a narcotic, and cannabis is not a narcotic. These substances tend to do something very different from producing sleep. They tend, instead, to produce a peculiar kind of wakefulness and a sharpening rather than a dimming of consciousness. So they must not be lumped in the same category as true narcotics.

Narcotics are also addictive. Alcohol is addictive, and the opiates are addictive. One can become physically dependent on them, and only with great difficulty can one shake them off. The same is true of tobacco. It is very difficult for a hardened smoker to drop the habit. I doubt, however, that tobacco is actually a narcotic in the sense of being sleep-inducing.

Our absurdly paranoid government agencies have not learned in fifty years the difference between narcotics and nonnarcotic drugs. Nor have they learned how to handle these problems. Despite the lessons of prohibition, the authorities still think that the only way to deal with dangerous narcotics is simply to suppress them, not realizing that this makes them all the more attractive. It also creates an enormous crime problem, which, without the suppression of drugs, would not exist. It is very difficult to suppress these things completely. You can suppress them a little bit, and you can pick out a few fall guys and make terrible examples of them by putting them in prison for an incredible number of years, but this only scratches the surface. When something illegal is really popular, there is no way to suppress it because all the hotels in the United States would not be sufficient to jail all the criminals involved. This approach has never worked. Why people don't learn from history is beyond my comprehension.

As people become aware that there are an enormous number of varieties of things that will produce psychedelic effects, the problem becomes much worse. In particular, such substances as LSD can be compressed into such small volumes that their detection is virtually impossible. So the moment these substances become a racket—something from which organized crime can make a good profit—the possibilities of manipulating the market become enormous. The real racket is the suppression of drugs. We have never really understood what control is, and we don't see the difference between controlling oneself and strangling oneself. In other words, a person who is a controlled automobile driver is certainly not a person who has no car or keeps his car locked in the garage. A very controlled dancer is certainly not a person who never dances. The control of things is not the suppression of them, but their use in a sensible and proper way. And this has not penetrated the consciousness of our authorities.

You cannot suppress mankind's fascination and curiosity about states of consciousness other than the normal. These things are eternally fascinating to human beings, and will always be pursued. Whether you think it is good or bad makes no difference. It will be done. At the present time, for example, if people want to experiment with LSD or mescaline or any consciousness-changing material, they are in a ridiculous situation. They cannot even pay a psychiatrist to sit with them and take care of them while they do it, because that would be illegal. What they will do is *not* have a psychiatrist or experienced person present. They will try it out all on their own without any preparation and endanger themselves, because drugs, under unfavorable circumstances and when used by people who do not have a good psychic balance, can bring about prolonged bouts of psychosis. With these substances, this can lead to a good deal of trouble. But the difficulty is that we are, as a culture, not prepared for the controlled use of these substances. That is why there is a panic and why our current method of dealing with drugs is probably worse than allowing them to circulate freely.

I would not for one moment advocate the free circulation of these substances so that anybody could go into a drugstore and buy them. But I think it would be better than total suppression because it is less destructive. But what we don't know is how to apply proper controls to the transformation of human consciousness by relatively easy means because we are not clear as to the role of these chemicals or the proper role of the physician. And this is something I want to consider.

In ancient times, there was no clear distinction between priests and physicians. An individual might be primarily a priest and secondarily a physician. Over time, the functions of priest and physician began to separate. The advent of scientific medicine was opposed by the Church, and therefore priests tended not to practice scientific medicine. The practitioners of scientific medicine, being other than priests, separated from religious professions. As medicine developed in the West, the deep concern of the physician became to preserve people from death—to be a healer—and the function of looking after death was abandoned to the priest and the minister. So when the doctor, in treating a patient, gives up hope of saving that life, he is out of his role. He doesn't know what to do beyond that point, and therefore the priest is summoned.

So the work of a doctor is curative throughout. He is, in all his activities, opposed to death and regards death as the enemy. This is, of course, not true of every individual physician. But it is true of medical ethics and of physicians generally. This means that people with terminal illnesses are being tortured—albeit with a good motive, but nonetheless tortured—by being kept alive in a state of near-mummification. We have come to believe that while there is life, there is hope, and that in the next few days there might be some amazing medical discovery that could cure the terminally ill. It would be a shame to let them die and not reap the benefit of such a cure. And yes, there always might be.

So the fact that the physician is, in general, out of his role and does not know what to do in the face of death has a very important connection with another aspect of the physician's trade: He does not know what to do with chemicals or drugs that do not have the function of healing a physical disease. In a way, all consciousness-expanding drugs have something to do with death because, as Jung pointed out, all spiritual disciplines are preparations for death. Every spiritual discipline involves a form of death—what is called "dying to oneself" or what the Christians call "dying daily"—and this is identified with the crucifixion of St. Paul. In the famous words of St. Paul, "I am crucified with Christ, yet I live. But not I, for it is Christ that lives in me." He also uses the phrase, "being baptized into Christ's death." That's all very funny language to the modern mind. But it is a commonplace of the spiritual disciplines that what you must do is die in the midst of life. You are born again a second time, and that death refers to the death of the ego.

You live behind the state of consciousness in which you thought you were no more than an isolated, individual center of consciousness. That perspective drops back, and in that sense you have died.

As an aid to that, spiritual disciplines often involve the contemplation of death. We think it is rather ghoulish nowadays, but monks used to keep skulls on their desks, and Buddhists meditate in graveyards. Hindu yogis meditate beside the burning funeral pyres on the banks of the Ganges, where they are always confronted with death, knowing this is going to happen to them.

Gurdjieff once said, "If anything would possibly save mankind from its idiocy, it would be the clearest possible recognition by every individual that he, and all others around him, are most certainly going to die." When this thought becomes perfectly clear to you, surprising becomes a source of intense joy and vitality. When you have accepted your own death in the midst of life, it means that you have let go of yourself, and you are therefore free. You are no longer plagued by worry and anxiety. You know that you are done for anyhow, so there is no need to fight constantly to protect yourself. What's the point? And it isn't just that people spend all their time doing something to really protect themselves, like taking out an insurance policy or eating properly. Instead it is what we do that doesn't cause any action at all: the constant inner worry that leads to no action except more worry. That is what is given up by a person who really knows that they are dead. So do you see that transcending yourself, going on beyond your ego, is the great preparation for death?

Now, if the medical profession takes the side of the ego against death—opposes death and regards death as the supreme evil—then the doctor really is out of his role at the bedside of a dying patient. And he also is out of his role when it comes to handling drugs that are not designed to heal sicknesses as we ordinarily define them.

But what really happens when someone develops a state of mind not considered to be psychologically normal? Sometimes a priest is called. But today, very few people, even churchgoing Christians, take priests seriously. When somebody in a good Christian family shows signs of mental derangement, the priest is very seldom called in. One calls in a psychiatrist. Why? Because he is a scientist, and, in our culture, the scientist has a greater reputation for magical power than do priests or ministers. We only call in the priest when all hope is abandoned.

Catholic or Anglican priests, by and large, are very used to handling death. They know what to do, and they come without any embarrassment, with the book open to the right place, and proceed to administer the last rites. And that is rather good, because here is a man who knows what to do and isn't flustered in the face of death. That in itself has a calming influence. However, a lot of people feel that this isn't really the way to handle death because they don't understand these last rites. So if the priest is called in only in desperation, this suggests that he does not have much power anyway. He may have power to do something with the Lord and the world beyond, but it is very doubtful he will be effective in this world.

Under such circumstances, both priest and physician need to take another look at death and rediscover the all-important fact that life without death has no value. Death, as Norman Brown pointed out in his book *Life Against Death*, "is what confers individuality upon us." It is your limits in time that constitute you, just as much as your limits in space. Death therefore always overshadows the whole of life, and life would have no meaning, no point, if it didn't have death to balance it. Life and death are the in-breath and out-breath, the coming and going, the rising and falling. They are mutually interdependent. Death is a very important and valuable thing that has been swept under the carpet.

So then, in a culture where priest and physician have become widely separated, the sudden bursting upon us of sacramental substances is an embarrassment to both. It is embarrassing to the priest for many reasons. Suppose we were to say that psychedelic substances are not the province of physicians and psychiatrists, but the province of the clergy. Everybody would throw up their hands and say, "These people have no scientific training. They don't know anything about neurology. They don't know anything about the subtle effects of these things on the human organism. How could they be responsible?" And, alas, that is true. The clergy have no training in neurology—so much the worse for them.

On the other hand, the psychiatrist and neurologist, with very few exceptions, have had no training in theology. And when most of them talk about theology, they reveal their abysmal ignorance of the whole matter.

So the issue falls right between the two schools. Although there are talented individuals who understand this sort of thing, there is no recognized class of people who might be called, for example, theo-botanists or theo-neurologists. We need to see the development of such a profession. Until we have it, we will be in a difficult situation.

How to deal with drugs, if you will, or chemicals that do not seem to have, as their primary use, the healing of a physical disease, poses an interesting problem. There is a sense in which these substances are medicine, rather than diet. A medicine is something you need when something is out of order, whereas a diet is what you live on permanently. (Of course, corrections in diet can have a medicinal effect.)

But surely there is a very true sense in which we can say that a world based on an egocentric consciousness is very seriously sick. Everybody knows why, and we can see all around us that we are stark-raving mad and are preparing to destroy ourselves. This is a sickness that needs some kind of remedy—maybe even a desperate remedy. The use of substances that would lift us out of the egocentric situation could therefore be considered medicine for a social disorder.

But again, I would say that substances used in that way should be used as medicine in the sense that they should not become diet. In this matter, everybody speaks for himself, but I have discovered that this is not the sort of thing you take very often, as you might go to church. It is something that you can take several times in gradually diminishing quantity. Beyond that, it is up to you to integrate your vision with everyday life.

However, there are other people who seem to think that the great thing to do is to start out with a little and then keep on going, making it bigger and bigger, as if they were looking for something that should lie at the end of the line. But then it becomes a diet, and that is getting hooked on medicine. Very rightly doctors don't like to hook you on medicine because the goal of a good doctor is to get rid of you as a chronic patient. He doesn't want people hanging on to him and always coming for help. He wants to set you back on your own feet, and that is an excellent principle.

In this area, the doctor really has something to say to the priest because priests tend, by and large, to want to keep you coming to church so that you will pay your dues and the church will prosper. So the more people they can get hooked on religion, the better. Now priests ought to learn from doctors and try to get rid of people by telling them their gospel, or whatever it is they have to say, and then saying, "Now you've had it, go away." If the priest did that, he would create a vacuum, and it would always be filled. The faster a doctor can get people out of his office, the sooner they go around and tell everybody, "This man cured me. I didn't have to go back." And the more people will come in. There are always plenty of sick people. So in the same way, the religious man ought to handle a huge turnover of people coming through and going away. Then he is really working.

But he should not get them hooked on the medicine of churches. There is a Latin expression that means "the Cross is the medicine of the world." But people get hung up on the cross. Jesus didn't get hung up. According to the Christian mythology, Jesus came alive again afterwards, if only for awhile. In the same way, if Christians really believed in the inner meaning of the doctrine, they wouldn't get hung up on the cross either, but embrace it only temporarily. "I am crucified with Christ, nevertheless I live."

So also, when it comes to the use of any technique whatsoever for spiritual awakening, whether it is yoga or LSD or religion, there is something to be learned from Buddha's symbol of the raft. The Buddha likened his method—his *Dharma*, or doctrine—to a raft. This method is also called a *yana*, or vehicle—hence the *Mahayana*, or big vehicle, and the *Hinayana*, or little vehicle. The raft takes you across the river: This shore is birth and death, and the other shore is liberation, or *nirvana*. You climb aboard the raft to cross the river. But when you get to the other shore, you leave the raft behind.

In much the same way, Zen Buddhism uses a technique: the *koan*, or meditation problem. It is like knocking at a door with a brick. When the door is opened, you don't carry the brick inside. You leave the brick behind.

Each of these techniques is a means, *upaya*, and each has as its objective the deliverance from the means. The Christian mystics speak of the highest state of contemplative prayer, or union with God, as a union without means. And I would extend the sense of the word *means* even to ecstasy. In other words, in the great religious traditions, ecstasy is not a final state. Ecstasy is an intermediate state. For example, in Zen, when the experience of *satori*, or awakening, comes about, there is a feeling of ecstasy. You feel as if you were walking on air, and you feel absolutely unobstructed. You feel as happy as a lark, and it is marvelous. But that in itself is only incidental.

A Zen proverb says, "A monk who has a satori goes to hell as straight as an arrow." In other words, to have it is to cling to it, and although you may think that the ecstasy is the important thing, it isn't. Ecstasy is an intermediate stage to bring you back to the point where you can see that everyday life—your ordinary mind, as they say in Zen—is the Buddha mind. Everyday life, just as it is, is the great thing, and there is no difference between that and the divine life.

However, so long as you think that there is a state of affairs in which you can say of the big thing—whether

it is God, nirvana, Brahma, the Divine, or the Tao—
"I've got it," you haven't. The moment you regard it as
some sort of object, as some sort of state or some sort of
thing that you can possess, you have pushed it away
from yourself. The one thing you can't lay your hands
on is you. You would never figure it out, not in a million
years, and you can't even find out who it is that wants to
find out. And whoever wants to find out who it is and
wants to find out, will never get at it. That's the thing. It
is the thing that is most close to you, as Francis
Thompson said, "Nearer is he than breathing, closer
than hands and feet."

What is absolutely central to you is that which
you can never make an object of knowledge, and so you
finally get to the point that you don't have to have anything, because you are it. You don't even need to insist
that you are it, because if you have to insist on that,
then you doubt it, and you will have to go around saying to yourself, "Be still and know that I am God." But
that's for beginners. When you really get at the end of
it, there isn't a trace. No means are left, no methods, no
getting hold of it. No meditation, no LSD—no nothing—because it is just the way it is.

To sum up: In the final analysis, all spiritual
awakenings involve something beyond the will and the
ego. You cannot do it yourself, so it makes little difference what you use to get there. Some ways are easier
than others. It's easier to use theo-botany, a divine
plant, than to bang your head against a brick wall. But
with the very ease of it, there is the danger that you may
neglect the discipline that must go with it. With "bang-
ing your head against a brick wall," at least you are sure
to know the danger before anything happens. The discipline is relatively easy to handle. Of course, as Aldous
Huxley once said, "To insist upon using the more ardu-

ous ways to attain the mystical state, is rather like burning down your farm house every time you want roast pork." The problem for us is that we don't have someone who integrates the role of priest and the role of physician, and the division into two roles has left both impoverished. So there is nobody who is really competent to deal with death or with preparation for death, and that creates a problem for us.

Finally, let me remind you that the most subtle danger in all these things—yoga or chemical methods—is fixation on ecstasy and not knowing how to go beyond ecstasy and beyond looking at the divine as something that one can personally possess.

PHILOSOPHY OF NATURE

CHAPTER SIX

C ontrary to popular belief, Americans are not materialists, as I have said before. We are not people who love material, and by and large our culture is devoted to the transformation of material into junk as rapidly as possible. God's own junkyard! Therefore, it's a very important lesson for a wealthy nation—and all Americans are colossally wealthy by the standards of the rest of the world—to see what happens to material in the hands of people who love it.

You might say that in Japan, and in China to a certain extent, the underlying philosophy of life is a sort of spiritual materialism. In the East, there is not the divorce between soul and body, between spirit and matter, between God and nature, that there is in the West. Therefore, there is not the same kind of contempt for material things.

We regard matter as something that gets in our way, something with limitations that are to be abolished as quickly as possible. We have bulldozers and every kind of technical device for knocking material out of the way, and we like to do as much to obliterate time and space as possible. We talk about killing time and getting from one place to another as fast as possible.

This is one of the great difficulties facing Japan. What is going to happen to Japan when it becomes the same place as California? In other words, you can take a streetcar from one end of town to another, and it's the same town. So, if you can take a jet plane from one city to another, then they're going to become the same place. To preserve the whole world from ultimate Los Angelization, we in the United States have to learn how to enjoy material and to be true materialists, instead of exploiters of material. This is one of the main reasons for exploring the philosophy of the Far East and how it relates to everyday life—to architecture, to gardens, to painting, and to rituals like the tea ceremony.

Basic to all of this is the philosophy of nature. The Japanese philosophy of nature is probably founded on the Chinese philosophy of nature, so we'll begin there.

To let the cat out of the bag right at the beginning: The basic assumption underlying Far Eastern and East Indian cultures is that the whole cosmos, the whole universe, is one being. It is not a collection of many things that floated together like a lot of flotsam and jetsam from the ends of space and just happened to end up forming this thing we call the universe. Easterners look at the world as one eternal activity, and that's the only real self you have. You are the works, and that thing we call you, the so-called "separate organism," is simply a manifestation of the whole thing. And this is not just a theory, it is a feeling that they have.

The great masters of the Far East and India, whatever sphere they're in, are fundamentally of this feeling that what you are is the thing that always was, is, and will be. And this eternal thing is playing the games called "Mr. Tocano," or "Mr. Lee," or "Mr. Mukapadya." These are special games it's playing, just like there's the fish game, the grass game, the bamboo game, and the pine tree game. These are all ways of saying, "Hello. Look at me. Here I am. It's me!" And everything is doing a dance, only it's doing it according to its own nature and the nature of the dance. The universe is fundamentally all these dances, whether human, fish, bird, cloud, sky, or star. They are all one fundamental dance or dancer. In Chinese, however, one doesn't distinguish the noun from the verb in the same way that we do. A noun can become a verb; a verb can become a noun. Now, that's a civilized culture!

Above all, an enlightened person in Eastern culture is one who knows that his so-called "separate personality," his ego, is an illusion. Illusion doesn't mean a bad thing; it just means a play. From the Latin word *ludere*, we get the English word illusion, and ludere means to play. The Sanskrit word *maya*, meaning illusion, also means magic, skill, art. This Sanskrit concept comes through China to Japan with the transmission of Buddhism.

The East Indian vision of the world as a maya, or as it is sometimes called in Sanskrit, *lila*, is also to play. So, all individual manifestations are games, dances, symphonies, and musical forms of the whole show. And the underlying belief is that everyone is the whole show.

But nature, as the word is used in the East, does not mean quite the same thing as it does in the West. In Chinese, the word we translate as nature is *tse-jan*, and it is made up of two characters. The first one means "of itself," and the second one means "so." What is so, of itself?

This is a rather difficult idea to translate into English. We might say "automatic," but that suggests something mechanical. This is something that is of itself so—what happens, what comes naturally. It is our sense of the word nature insofar as it means to be natural, to act in accordance with one's nature, not to strive for things, not to force things. When your hair grows, it grows without your telling it to do so, and you don't have to force it to grow. In the same way, your eyes, whether they are blue or brown, color themselves, and you don't tell them how to do it. When your bones grow a certain way, they do it all of themselves.

I remember a Zen master who taught in New York. He was a beautiful man, and his name was Mr. Sasaki. One evening, he was sitting in his golden robes, in a very formal thronelike chair with a fan in his hand. He had one of those fly whisks made of a white horse's tail. He was looking very dignified, with incense burning on the table in front of him. There was a little desk and on it was one of the scriptures that he was explaining. He said, "All nature has no purpose. Purposelessness most fundamental principle of Buddhism; purposelessness. Ahhh, when you drop fart, you don't say, 'At nine o'clock I dropped fart.' It just happens."

It is fundamental to this idea of nature that the world has no boss. This is very important, especially if you're going to understand Shinto. We translate *kami*, or *shin*, as God, but it's not God in that sense. God, in the common Western meaning of the word, means "the controller," "the boss of the world." And the model that we use for nature tends to be the model of the carpenter or potter or king. Just as the carpenter takes wood and makes a table out of it or as the potter takes inert clay and evokes a form in it or as the king tells people what order they shall move in and how they shall behave, it is ingrained in the Western mind to think that the universe is a behavior that is responding to somebody in charge— somebody who understands it all.

When I was a little boy, I used to ask my mother many questions. Sometimes she'd get fed up with me and say, "My dear, there are some things in this life that we are just not meant to know."

And so I said, "Well, what about it? Will we ever know?"

"Yes," she said. "When you die and you go to Heaven, God will make it all clear."

And I used to think that maybe, on wet afternoons in Heaven, we'd all sit around God's throne and say, "Oh, Heavenly Father, why are the leaves green?" And he would say, "Because of the chlorophyll!" And we would say, "Oh!"

Well, that idea—of the world as an artifact—could prompt a child in our culture to ask his mother, "How was I made?" And the question seems very natural. So when it's explained that God made you, the child naturally goes on and says, "But who made God?"

However, I don't think a Chinese child would ask the question, "How was I made?" And this is because the Chinese mind does not look at the world of nature as something manufactured, but rather grown. The character for coming into being in Chinese is based on the symbol of a growing plant, and growing and making are two different things. When you make something, you assemble parts or you take a piece of wood and you carve it, working gradually from the outside inward, cutting away until you've got the shape you want.

But when you watch something grow, it isn't like that. If you see, for example, a fast-motion movie of a rose growing, you will see that the process goes from the inside to the outside. It is, as it were, something expanding from the center. And far from being an addition of parts, it all moves together and grows out of itself all at once. The same is true when you watch the formation of crystals or a photographic plate being developed. Suddenly, all over the area of the plate, all over the field, the photo appears.

So the world as a self-generating organism does not obey laws in our sense of "the laws of nature," and in Chinese philosophy there is no difference between the *Tao* (in Japanese, *do*), the way or power of nature, and the things in nature. Everything is said to have its own Tao, from which it acts according to its own nature. Of course, here I am using "nature" to mean the character or qualities of a thing and not something distinct from man.

When I stir up the air with a fan, it isn't simply that the air obeys the fan. There wouldn't even be a fan in my hand unless there were air around. So unless there is air, there is no fan. The air brings the fan into being as much as the fan brings the air into being. Because the Taoists see the unity implied in the interdependence of things, they don't think of things as obeying all the time, of masters and slaves, of lords and servants.

Lao-tzu, who is supposed to have written the *Tao Te Ching*, the fundamental book of Taoist philosophy, is said to have lived in China around the time of Confucius. In his book, he wrote, "The great Tao flows everywhere, to the left and to the right. It loves and nourishes all things, but does not lord it over them. And

when merits are attained, it makes no claim to them."
Now it seems probable that this book was actually a collection of the wisdom of the day. And if this is the way nature is run, why not the government as well? By letting everything follow its course, the skillful man or woman—and also the skillful ruler—interferes as little as possible with the course of things.

Of course, for the reasons noted above, you can't help but interfere a little. Every time you look at something, you change it. Your very existence is, in a way, an interference, and if you think of yourself as something separate from the rest of the world, then you will think in terms of interference and noninterference. But if you know that you're not separate from it, that you are just as much in and of nature as the wind or the clouds, then who is it that interferes?

The same principle is seen in the notion that life is most skillfully lived when one sails a boat rather than rowing it. It's more intelligent to sail than to row. With oars I have to use my muscles and my effort to drag myself along the water. But with a sail, I let the wind do the work for me. And it is more skillful still when I learn to tack and let the wind blow me against the direction of the wind.

That balance of participation is the whole philosophy of the Tao. It's called, in Chinese, *wu wei*; *wu* is "non," and *wei* is "striving." *Mui* is the Japanese version of this concept. In Japanese, *mu* is the Chinese wu, and so in this context becomes *mui*, as distinct from *ui*. Ui means to use effort, that is, to go against the grain, to force things. So together they mean not to go against the grain, that is, to go with the grain. If you travel through Japan, you will see around you, in every direction, examples of mui, of the intelligent handling of nature so as to go with it rather than against it.

For example, the famous art of judo is entirely based on this principle. When you are attacked, you don't simply oppose the force used against you. Instead, you go in the same direction as the attack is headed, and lead it to its own downfall. This is the same strategy seen in the way a willow tree survives the winter. Nearby there is a strong pine tree that has a tough branch that reaches out, flexing its muscles. Then the snow piles up and up, and this unyielding branch holds a huge weight of snow. It cracks. However, the willow tree has a springy, supple branch, and when a little snow comes on it the branch just goes down. The snow falls off, and the branch goes up again.

Lao-tzu said, "Man, at his birth, is supple and tender. But in death, he is rigid and hard. Plants when they are young, are soft and supple. But in death, they are brittle and hard. So, suppleness and tenderness are the characteristics of life, and rigidity and hardness the characteristics of death." He made many references to water and said, "Of all things in the world, nothing is more soft than water, and yet it wears away the hardest rocks. Furthermore, water is humble, it always seeks the lowest level, which men abhor. But eventually, water overcomes everything in its path."

When you watch water take the line of least resistance and you see, for example, water poured out on the ground, you will see it projecting fingers from itself. Some of those fingers stop, but one finger goes on, because it has found the lowest level. Now, you might say, "Oh, but that's not the water. The water didn't do anything. That's just the contours of the land, and because of the contours of the land, the water goes where the land makes it go." But think again. Isn't it also the nature of water that makes it go?

I will never forget that once, when I was out in the countryside, a piece of thistledown flew out of the blue.

It came right down to me, and I put out a finger, and I caught it by one of its little tendrils. Then it behaved just like a daddy-longlegs; you know, when you catch one by a leg it naturally struggles to get away. Well, this little thing behaved just like that, and I thought, "It is just the wind doing that. It only appears as if the thistledown is doing that." But then I thought again, "It is the wind, yes, but it's also this thistledown that had the intelligence to grow itself so as to use the wind to help it get away." That little structure of thistledown exhibits a high form of intelligence, just as surely as the construction of a house that follows the contours of the land is a manifestation of a high level of human intelligence. But the thistledown is using the wind instead of the slope.

In much the same way, the water uses the conformations of the ground to get away. Water isn't just dead stuff. It's not just being pushed around. In fact, nothing is being pushed around in the Chinese view of nature. What they mean by nature is something that happens of itself; it has no boss. Nobody is giving orders, and so nobody is obeying orders. That leads further to an entirely different conception of cause and effect. Cause and effect is based on giving orders. When you say, "Something made this happen," you are saying it had to happen because of what happened before. But the Chinese don't think like that. Their concept, which does duty for our idea of causality, is called "mutual arising."

As an example, let's consider the relationship between the back and the front of anything. Is the back the cause of the front, or is the front the cause of the back? What a silly question! If things don't have fronts, then they can't have backs. If they don't have backs, they can't have fronts. Front and back always go together; that is to say, they come into being together. And so, in just the same way as the front and the back arise together, Taoist philosophy sees everything in the world arising together.

This is called the philosophy of mutual interpenetration—in Japanese, *gigi muge*—and it goes way back in history to the Chinese idea of nature. To look at it very simply, let us suppose that you had never seen a cat, and one day you were looking through a very narrow slit in a fence, and a cat walked by. First you would see the cat's head. Then there's a rather nondescript fuzzy interval, and then a tail follows. And you say, "Marvelous!" Then the cat turns around and walks back. You see the head, and then after a little interval, the tail. You might say, "My! That's just incredible! The head caused the tail." The cat then turns around and walks back, and again you see first the head and then the tail. So you say, "This has some regularity, and there must be some order in this phenomenon. Whenever I see the thing that I've labeled head, I then see the thing I've labeled tail. Therefore, where there is an event that I call 'head' and it's invariably followed by another event that I call 'tail,' obviously the head is the cause, and the tail is the effect."

We think that way about everything. But if you suddenly widened the crack in the fence, you would see that the head and the tail are all one cat. Like everything else that comes into being naturally, a cat is born with a head and a tail. In exactly the same way, the events that we seem to call "separate" are really all one event. But we chop it into pieces to describe it, just as we say, "The head of the cat and the tail of the cat," although it's all one head-tail cat. We've chopped it to pieces in order to describe it, but then we forget that we did that. We try to explain how the pieces fit together. So we have invented a myth called "causality" in order to explain how they do fit together.

We chop the world into bits as a matter of intellectual convenience. However, our world is very wiggly through and through, and you will notice how people, although they hold up models of symmetry as seen in most houses, love the wigglyness in their garden. Nature is fundamentally wiggly.

I remember as a child wondering why Chinese houses all had curved roofs, and why all the people in the landscapes looked more wiggly than ours. Finally I figured out that this is because they see that the world is wiggly! We say, "Now, what can you do with a wiggly world? You've got to straighten it out!" Always, our initial solution is to try and straighten things out.

Of course people are very wiggly indeed. It is only because we all appear pretty much the same that we look regular. We have two eyes, one nose, one mouth, two ears, and so on. We look regular, so we make sense. But if somebody had never seen a person before, he might ask, "What is this extraordinarily wiggly phenomenon? It seems to wiggle all over the place!"

One of the wiggliest things in the world is a fish. Somebody once found out they could use a net and catch a fish. Then they thought of an even better idea than that: They could catch the world with a net and use it to make sense of a wiggly world. But what happens if you hang up a net in front of the world and look through it? You can count the wiggles by saying, this wiggle goes so many holes up, so many holes down, and so many holes across. It goes so many to the left and so many to the right. But what do you end up with? What you have as a result of this exercise is a calculus. Your net breaks up the world into countable bits.

In the same way, a bit is a bite of something, just as when you go to eat chicken, you can't swallow the whole chicken at once. To eat it you have to cut it into bites. But you don't get a cut-up fryer out of the egg. So in the same way the real universe has no bits. It's all one thing; it's not a lot of things. In order to digest it with your mind, which thinks of one thing at a time, you have to construct a calculus. So you chop the universe into bits, and you think about it, and talk about it one bit at a time.

You can see this whole page at once, but if you want to talk about it, you have to talk about it word by word, idea by idea, and bit by bit.

So to describe things, you go into all the details. But how does one select which details? Well now, if you don't realize that's what you've done, that you've "bitted" the world in order to think about it when it isn't really bitted at all, then you have troubles. Not only do you have to explain how the bits go together, but in order to explain how they connect with each other you have to invent all sorts of ghosts. Some of these ghosts are called "cause and effect," influences used to explain things. Indeed you may ask, "How do I influence you?" But what does this really mean? These influences—the ghosts and spooks we regard as things—only come into being if we forget that we made the initial step of breaking the unity into pieces in order to discuss it. That is, they are a part of the illusion.

Stepping back, we have these basic principles to consider. The world as nature, what happens of itself, is looked upon as a living organism. It doesn't have a boss because things are not behaving in response to something that pushes them around. They are just behaving, and it's all one big behavior. However, if you want to look at it from certain points of view, you can see it as if something else were making something happen, just as we looked at the cat through the slit in the fence. But you only see the parts because you divide the thing up.

This might lead you to ask, "In Chinese philosophy, is nature chaotic? Is there really no law?" There is no Chinese word that means the law of nature. The only word in Chinese that means law—*tse*—is a character that represents a cauldron with a knife beside it. It goes back to very ancient times, when a certain emperor made laws for the people. He had the laws etched on the sacrificial cauldrons so that when the people brought the sacrifices they would read what was written on the cauldrons. But the sages, who were of a Taoist persuasion during the time that this emperor lived, said, "You shouldn't have done that, Sir, because the moment the people know what the law is, they become a little devious. And they'll say, 'Well now, did you really mean that precisely or did you mean this?' The next thing you know, they will find a way to wrangle around it." So they said that the nature of nature, Tao, is *wu-tse*, which means lawless.

But although we say that nature is lawless, this is not to say it is chaotic. The Chinese word for the order in nature is *li*. In Japanese, it is *ri*. Li is a curious word that originally meant "the markings in jade, the grain in wood, or the fiber in muscle." Now, when you look at jade and you see these wonderful, mottled markings, you know that somehow these marking are not chaotic, although you can't explain why. And when you look at the patterns of clouds or the bubbles of foam on the water, it's astounding, because they never make an aesthetic mistake.

Look at the stars. They are not arranged; instead they seem to be scattered through the heavens like sea spray. Yet you could never criticize stars for displaying poor taste, any more than you could criticize mountain ranges for having awkward proportions. These designs are spontaneous, and yet they demonstrate the wiggly patterns of nature that are quite different from anything you would call a mess. We can't quite put our finger on what the difference is between the two, but we certainly can see the difference between a tide pool and an ashtray full of garbage. We may not be able to define the difference, but we know they are different.

If you could define aesthetic beauty, however, it would probably cease to be interesting. That is, if we had a way of capturing it and a method that would automatically produce great artists—and anybody could go to school and become a great artist—art would soon become the most boring kind of expression. But precisely because you don't know how it's done, that gives spontaneous art a level of excitement.

And so it is with the philosophy of nature. There is no formula, no tse or rule according to which all this happens. And yet it's not a mess. So, this idea of li, or organic pattern, is the word that they use for the order of nature. Instead of our idea of law, where the things are obeying something, they are not obeying a God in the sense of a governor. They are not following principles, like a streetcar that follows along the track.

Do you know that limerick about the streetcar?

There was a young man who said, "Damn!
For it certainly seems that I am
    A creature that moves
    In determinate grooves.
I'm not even a bus, I'm a tram!"

So that idea of the iron rails, along which the course of life goes, is absent in the East. And that accounts for a certain humanism that is very present in these cultures. The people in the Far East, and particularly in China and Japan, never feel guilty. They may feel ashamed because they have transgressed social requirements, but they do not have the sense of guilt that we generally equate with sinfulness. They don't feel, as with the idea of original sin, that you are guilty because you owe your existence to the Lord God—or perhaps you were a mistake anyway! They don't feel that. They have social shame, but not metaphysical guilt, and that leads to a great relaxation. You can feel it, if you're sensitive, just walking around the streets. You realize that these people have not been tarred with that terrible monotheistic brush that gives one the sense of guilt.

Instead they work on the supposition that human nature, like all nature, although it consists of the passions as much as the virtues, is essentially good. In Chinese the word *un* means human-heartedness, or humanness, but not in the sense of being humane out of a kind of necessity, but of being human. So when I say, "Oh, he's a great human being," I mean he's the kind of person who's not a stuffed shirt, who is able to come off it, who can talk with me as a person, and who recognizes that he is a rascal, too. And so when a man, for example, affectionately calls a friend, "you old bastard," this is a term of endearment, because he knows that "the old bastard" shares with him what I call the "element of irreducible rascality" that we all have.

So then, if a person has this attitude, he is never going to be an overbearing goody-goody. Confucius said, "Goody-goodies are the thieves of virtue." Because the philosophy of the goody-goody is, "If I am right, then you are wrong, and we will get into a fight. What I am is a crusader against the wrong, and I'm going to obliterate you, or I'm going to demand your unconditional surrender." But if I say, "No, I'm not right, and you're not wrong, but I happen to want to win. You know, you've got the most beautiful temples and I'm going to fight you for them." But if I had done that, I would be very careful not to destroy the temples.

However in modern warfare we don't care. The only people who are safe are in the air force, because they are way up there. The women and children will be gone, because they can be frizzled with a Hiroshima bomb. But we in the plane will be safe. Now this is inhuman because we are fighting for ideology instead of for practical things like food, and for possessions, and for greed.

So this is why the Chinese recognize both sides of human nature, and a Confucian would say he trusts human passions more than he trusts human virtues: righteousness, goodness, principles, and all that highfalutin abstraction. Let's get down to earth, let's come off it. And this, then, is why there is a kind of man in whom trust is put, because he recognizes the kind of nature that human nature is. If you are like the Christians who don't trust human nature—who say, "It's fallen, it's evil, it's perverse"—that puts you in a very funny position. If you say, "Human nature is not to be trusted," then you can't even trust the fact that you don't trust it! And do you see where you'll end up?

Now, it's true that human nature is not always trustworthy, but you must proceed on the gamble that it's trustworthy most of the time, or at least 51 percent of the time. Because if you don't, what's your alternative? You have to have a police state, and everybody has to be watched and controlled. But then who's going to watch the police? So, you end up the way they did in China just before 250 B.C. when there was the Ch'in Dynasty that lasted fifteen years. The emperor decided that everything would be completely controlled in order to make his dynasty last for a thousand years. In the process, he made a mess. So the Han Dynasty, which lasted from 250 B.C. to 250 A.D., came into being, and the first thing they did was abolish all laws, except those about elementary violence and robbery. But all of the complexity of law was removed, and historically the Han Dynasty marked the height of Chinese civilization. It was a period of real peace and great sophistication. It was China's Golden Age, although I may be oversimplifying it a bit, as all historians do.

This marvelous reign was based on the whole idea of the humanism of the Far East, recognizing that although human beings are scalawags, they are no more so than cats and dogs and birds. So you must trust human nature, because if you can't, you're apt to starve.

ALAN WATTS AUDIO COLLECTIONS
Original Live Recordings
from Electronic University

USING STATE-OF-THE-ART technology, Electronic University has captured and enhanced the natural sound from the original recordings so that the insights from one of this century's most notable philosophers come through as clearly as the day Alan Watts first spoke them.

The Tao of Philosophy — Volume I
ISBN 1-882435-10-9

❏ *Slices of Wisdom*—Notable segments drawn from the first thirteen weeks of the *Love of Wisdom* public radio series. (29 min.)

❏ *Images of God*—Watts explores the metaphysics underlying feminine symbolism in images of the divine throughout the world, in which "the deep" and "the dark" are recognized as the unifying ground of being. (29 min.)

❏ *Sense of Nonsense*—Recorded live on KPFA, this popular program is a delightful excursion into the essential purposelessness of life. (29 min.)

❏ *Coincidence of Opposites*—Just as the purpose of dancing is not to arrive at a certain place on the floor, life has no concrete goal to be achieved. (29 min.)

❏ *Seeing Through the Net*—In a sparkling 1969 talk to IBM systems engineers, Watts describes the "net" of perception we throw over reality, and the contrasting perceptions of "prickles" and "goo." (58 min.)

The Tao of Philosophy — Volume II
ISBN 1-882435-11-7

❏ *Myth of Myself*—What do we mean when we use the word *I*? Could self-image be the barrier to knowing who and what we really are? (42 min.)

❏ *Man and Nature*—Western culture sees the world as a mechanical system, while Eastern philosophies see it as an all-encompassing organic process. Just as an apple tree "apples," the earth "peoples," and we are not so much born into this world as grown out of it. (56 min.)

❏ *Symbols and Meaning*—As symbols, words point to things they represent, and thus have meaning. By contrast, life itself does not stand for anything else and therefore has no meaning in the usual sense. (29 min.)

❏ *Limits of Language*—Watts suggests that language may alter our view of reality, and by knowing the limits of language we can move on to the unspeakable. (29 min.)

The Philosophies of Asia — Volume I
ISBN 1-882435-12-5

❏ *The Relevance of Oriental Philosophy*—Alan Watts looks at Eastern thought in contrast with the religions of the Western world. Chinese and Indian models are used to point out how we can better understand our own culture by contrasting it with others. (56 min.)

❏ *The Mythology of Hinduism*—An engaging overview of the Hindu perspective on the universe, its theory of time, and the concept of an underlying godhead that is dreaming all of us. (54 min.)

❏ *Eco-Zen*—Speaking before a college audience, Watts points out that "ecological awareness" and "mystical experience" are different ways of saying the same thing. (29 min.)

❏ *Swallowing a Ball of Hot Iron*—Continuing an introduction toward the understanding of Zen Buddhism, Watts describes the essential unity of the organism and its environment. (29 min.)

The Philosophies of Asia — Volume II
ISBN 1-882435-13-3

❏ *Intellectual Yoga*—In a lively discussion of the intellect as a path to one's enlightenment, Watts observes that "it is amazing how many things there are that aren't so." (42 min.)

❏ *Introduction to Buddhism*—Buddhism is traced from its origins in India to China, and then on to Japan. Along the way Watts brings to life one of the world's great religious traditions in its many forms, from the Theravada school to contemporary Zen. (58 min.)

❏ *The Taoist Way of Karma I*—The word *karma* literally means "doing," and is thus "your doing" or action. Taoism suggests a spontaneous course of action in accord with the current and grain of nature. (29 min.)

❏ *The Taoist Way of Karma II*—By following the Tao, or course of nature, one comes into harmony with the world and drops out of the cycles of karma perpetuated by our attempts to control destiny. (29 min.)

Myth and Religion

Each of these six controversial lectures challenges listeners to go beyond their usual mindsets to startling revelations about our most deep-rooted intellectual constructs. Not for the faint of heart!

❏ Not What Should Be, Not What Might Be, But What Is! (58 min.)

❏ Spiritual Authority (58 min.)

❏ Jesus: His Religion, or the Religion About Him? (58 min.)

❏ Democracy in the Kingdom of Heaven (58 min.)

❏ Image of Man (58 min.)

❏ Religion and Sexuality (58 min.)

Buddhism —The Religion of No-Religion

In a variety of settings from Kyoto to Sausalito, Alan Watts joyfully takes us on a journey to Buddhism, from its roots in India to the explosion of interest in Zen and the Tibetan tradition in the West.

❏ The Journey from India I (29 min.)
❏ The Journey from India II (29 min.)
❏ Buddhism as Dialogue (58 min.)
❏ Following the Middle Way (58 min.)

❏ Religion of No-Religion (58 min.)
❏ Wisdom of the Mountains (58 min.)
❏ Transcending Duality (29 min.)
❏ Diamond Web (29 min.)

Counter-Culture Series

❏ **Eastern and Western Zen**—Zen Stories (50 min.); Uncarved Block, Unbleached Silk (44 min.); Biting the Iron Bull (45 min.); Swimming Headless (51 min.); Wisdom on the Ridiculous (46 min.); Zen Bones (59 min.)

❏ **Philosophy and Society**—Veil of Thoughts (56 min.); Divine Madness (58 min.); We as Organism (58 min.); What Is Reality? (50 min.); Mysticism and Morality (58 min.); On Being God (60 min.)

❏ **Comparative Philosophy**—From Time to Eternity (55 min.); The Cosmic Drama (58 min.); Philosophy of Nature (50 min.); Spectrum of Love (58 min.); Game of Yes and No (50 min.); The Smell of Burnt Almonds (58 min.)

THE TAO OF PHILOSOPHY, VOLUMES I & II and THE PHILOSOPHIES OF ASIA, VOLUMES I & II each consist of three audio cassettes in an attractive bookshelf binder. The price for each volume is $29.95. Please add $3.00 per item for shipping.

MYTH AND RELIGION, BUDDHISM, PHILOSOPHY AND SOCIETY, EASTERN AND WESTERN ZEN, and COMPARATIVE PHILOSOPHY each consist of six audio cassettes in an attractive bookshelf binder. The regular list price for each series is $59.95. However, you may select any two series for $100, or all 42 tapes for $300.

Please add $3.00 per set for priority mail, $12.00 per set for overnight mail, or $8.00 per set for overseas shipping. Visa, MasterCard, and American Express accepted. To order, please call or write:

Electronic University
Post Office Box 2309
San Anselmo, CA 94979
Phone/Fax (800) 969-2887

Other Books in The "Love of Wisdom" Library

Each book consists of an introduction by Mark Watts and the edited transcripts of lectures given by Alan Watts.

Each book is $4^{3/4}$ x $8^{1/2}$ • Hardcover • U.S. $16.95

BUDDHISM: THE RELIGION OF NO-RELIGION

In this dynamic series of lectures, Alan Watts takes us on an exploration of Buddhism, from its roots in India to the explosion of interest in Zen and the Tibetan tradition in the West.
112 pages • 0 8048 3056 8

MYTH AND RELIGION

Although he is best known as a masterful interpreter of Eastern thought, Alan Watts is also recognized as a brilliant commentator on Judeo-Christian traditions.
128 pages • 0 8048 3055 X

THE PHILOSOPHIES OF ASIA

This book combines the transcripts of eight talks by Alan Watts from 1965 to 1972. Topics range from the relevance of Oriental philosophy to discussions of Hinduism, Yoga, Zen, Buddhism, and Taoism.
128 pages • 0 8048 3051 7

THE TAO OF PHILOSOPHY

This book covers the edited transcripts of eight talks from 1960 to 1973, offering Watts's insights on philosophical topics, reflecting his underlying appreciation for the wisdom inherent in the course and current of nature.
128 pages • 0 8048 3052 5

For a complete catalog call or write to:
Charles E. Tuttle Co., Inc.
RR1 Box 231-5
North Clarendon, VT 05759-9700
phone: (802) 773-8930
fax: (802) 773-6993
or call toll free: (800) 526-2778